CONTENTS

J William.

GOOD NEWS IN OUR TIMES
The Gospel and Contemporary Cultures

Report of the Mission Theological Advisory Group
of the Board of Mission of the General Synod
of the Church of England

GS 980

CHURCH HOUSE PUBLISHING
Church House, Great Smith Street, London SW1P 3NZ

ISBN 0 7151 5529 6

Published 1991 for the Board of Mission of the General Synod
of the Church of England by Church House Publishing

GS 980

© *The Central Board of Finance of the Church of England 1991*

Printed in England by Rapier Press Ltd.

INTRODUCTION

Any Group, such as our Mission Theological Advisory Group (MTAG), set up to respond to questions about mission in our times, has to recognise how the expression of our faith is influenced by the society to which we belong. We have to listen to the words of Jesus and experience the love of God and his demands on us within our own circumstances, so that we are often more like our immediate neighbours than our fellow-Christians of other cultures. But we are also uncomfortable with this and recognise that Christ's call and the cost of discipleship should, whenever necessary, have the overriding claim on our loyalties.

Looking at Christians in other parts of the world today and Christians at other times in history we may ask, 'what is it that links us together?' 'what do we have in common?' 'what is the essential Gospel that we all share?' 'how can we best put it into words?'

This Report concludes that just as the message of God to the Jewish people came through various cultures and as Jesus revealed God in a particular time and place, so the Gospel is not an 'abstract reality', but rather 'a shared experience to be lived'. In any group we look for 'the authentic Gospel ring', even when it is hard to distinguish it from other things. Part A of this Report ends with an attempt to express in contemporary terms certain essentials of the Gospel. We have called them 'Ten Signs of Authenticity'. They may help us to test contemporary claims that the Gospel is being lived and also may enable us to see where God is at work in the world.

Consistent with its theory, the Report gives many examples of contemporary British life both in society and the Church. It attempts to avoid simplistic or slick comments about them. We are sensitive to charges of cultural aggression and exclusivism, yet we seek to clarify the choices before the Church and to ask the hard questions which can clear the way for effective evangelism. How far should our priority be

(a) to serve society as it is, or
(b) to challenge the assumptions and behaviour of society, or
(c) to evangelise the individual and society by whatever means may be available?

We conclude in Part B that some will prefer one approach above another and that the aims need not be competitive. We look at examples both in this section and the next of what different Christians are doing and what their choices involve.

If the Report errs on the side of raising questions and of being over-cautious about solutions, it nevertheless in the third section addresses itself directly to such practical questions as baptismal policy, worship norms, Church structures and growth, leadership patterns and authentic discipleship. Some readers may prefer to start with this section before they turn to the other two. No universal blueprint can be discovered to solve all the dilemmas. Rather a theological tool-kit is offered to aid the task of constructing strategies and structures for each locality.

To confine such a huge subject and the mass of details, submissions and investigations to a manageable-sized report has been no easy task. The group is therefore extremely grateful to Mr Colin Alves who, on retirement as General Secretary of the National Society and the Board of Education, generously undertook to re-order the Report into what is substantially its present form.

Two obvious omissions in the report need comment. We were obliged to leave discussion of the rural Church until after the publication of *Faith in the Countryside*. And when faced with the choice of an illustration of a Gospel-culture issue from overseas or from Britain we more often chose the latter to make the point that the issues are on our doorstep. However, a significant percentage of our Group have strong links with the world church and ensured that the insights resulting from these links were formative in our work. In the Decade of Evangelism we look forward to the help which partners in the Church outside Britain will bring to us.

This Report is commended in the hope that through greater awareness of the cultural issues readers will begin to have greater confidence in perceiving and sharing the essential Gospel.

Philip King
Acting Chairman
April, 1991

Part A

The Gospel
in the Midst of Culture

Chapter 1

HOW DO WE DISCOVER THE CONTENT OF THE GOSPEL MESSAGE?

The source of the Gospel

1 The Bible is a collection of books which is both divine and human in its origin. We have to remember this in order to understand and appreciate its message. The writers were moved by the Holy Spirit (II Peter 1.21) and they 'spoke from God', but the way in which they spoke depended on their personalities, gifts and circumstances. That is one reason why we have four distinctive accounts of the life of Jesus, each one displaying plenty of evidence of the particular interests of its author. That is also why the subject matter and vocabulary of the letters in the New Testament vary from one to another; each author relates in his own way different facets of the Gospel to specific situations.

The writer's cultural setting

2 If we are to do justice to the way in which God's revelation has come to us through ordinary human beings, we must make full allowance for the fact that the people involved were immersed in their own particular culture and were speaking and writing out of a specific context. What belongs to the culture of the Biblical writers is sometimes easily distinguishable from what has validity across time. Hardly any Christians today would believe it was enough to say to owners of slaves 'Treat them well' and leave it at that. Not many would insist that women must cover their heads while praying. Few would claim that any prophetic message we have to deliver becomes more forceful if we first deface ourselves with sackcloth and ashes.

3 Jesus' teaching itself seemed to imply that certain cultural forms from the past (e.g. the use of sackcloth and ashes) are not an essential part of the true service of God. But does this apply to *all* such traditions? Paul instructed each congregation to take steps to support its widows. Should congregations *still* be expected to do this, or was that simply an aspect of Paul's immediate cultural setting which has no significance for us today and should therefore be ignored? We must tread carefully

here. In order that we may hear the full implications of the original message for our times we have to give due attention to those cultural aspects of its context which may not apply directly to us. For example, Jesus told his disciples to wash each other's feet. In what sense was that teaching meant for us? Was it in fact any easier for his immediate disciples to take that command literally than it is for us, or were they, like us perhaps, meant to take that instruction only symbolically? Questions like this are not always easy to answer, but the first step to finding answers is to recognise that the questions exist.

The writer's chosen form of expression
4 God has chosen to reveal himself and his will for the world through the full range of human characteristics. His revelation is expressed through a rich diversity of language and a wide variety of literary forms, such as stories, poetry, laws, parables, proverbs, drama, speeches and symbols. The ways in which both the language and the forms are used are common to the means by which human beings have communicated with one another down the ages and across the globe. They belong to a common, yet diverse, human heritage which enables and enriches our ability to share ideas and experiences and to tell others of the events which have happened to us.

5 It is because of this rich diversity of human forms of communication within the Bible that it is mistaken to try to understand every part of it in the same way. It leads to absurd conclusions to interpret every passage literally. One of the most basic principles of interpretation is to explore the *intention* of the writer both within the particular forms of expression he has chosen to use and within the cultural context of his own situation. We are almost certain to pervert the sense of the text if we ignore this rule.

The needs and assumptions of the reader
6 But it is not only the intention of the *writer* we have to explore within his own cultural setting. We also have to be aware of what we ourselves bring to the process of interpreting the text. Whenever we open the Bible to read it, for whatever purpose, we come to the text as people who have already been moulded and shaped by a whole set of assumptions, attitudes and experiences which inevitably will influence deeply what we find within its pages. Many examples could be given of ways in which political opinions, educational backgrounds, and minority status in unsympathetic cultural environments have caused Christians,

perhaps unconsciously, to focus on particular aspects of the Biblical message while filtering out others.

7 Christians have long discussed among themselves the meaning of 'justice'. Those who feel deeply the desperate plight of the poor will inevitably emphasise heavily the way in which the Scriptures stress the place of 'fairness' within the structures of society (distributive justice). They will call attention to the Sabbath and Jubilee Laws of the Old Testament and the prophetic texts which denounce the practices of bonded labour and the expropriation of land, houses and livelihood. On the other hand, those who give more significance to the importance of individual integrity are inclined to stress the Scriptures' insistence upon correct personal behaviour (retributive justice), drawing particular attention to those passages which demand a high level of individual honesty between people. When these differing approaches are then transmitted to current economic and political life we tend to find the first group advocating a policy of enforced redistribution of wealth, whilst the second group commend freedom within the market to create wealth along with a political and legal system freed from corruption. Both groups are quite convinced that they have full Scriptural authority for their particular political programme.

8 This example is one of many and shows how those who read the Bible do so with assumptions which have been influenced by their circumstances and experience. These assumptions determine what they believe the law, the prophets and the gospels are actually saying, they also determine the relative importance given to the message of the Old Testament and to that of the New, and also how far the Old is to be consciously interpreted in the light of the New.

The Word made Flesh
9 Care is needed to appreciate the way in which the Biblical text and our personal context should interact. Just as the original writers were immersed in their culture and situation, so too are we. Just as God's word to them came in the midst of a particular reality, so through them it comes to us in our very different set of circumstances. Thus it is inevitable that our experiences will colour what we read and the way we read it. That fact should not alarm us. On the contrary we should recognise that one of the basic tenets of the Christian faith is that God is among us and in the particular events of history. God's relations with his world are not those of a 'visitor', as in the tales of the old Greek or

Norse gods. 'The Word was made flesh', and God is still to be found *in* our various and differing situations. If we try to remove ourselves from our own context when trying to discover what God's message for us might be then we run a great risk of distorting that message. Of course we must recognise that our personal context produces within us biases and prejudices and that these may, on occasions, hinder rather than help a legitimate reading of the text. We must equally recognise, however, that if we seek only to read the text through the eyes of the first century disciples then we are very likely to miss what God is trying to say to us today.

Key questions
10   Two questions follow on from these considerations:

(a)   *What is God wanting to show us in our situation and asking us to share with those around us?*

One of the responsibilities of being the Church is to seek to enable God's word to be heard, and be understood as such, by others. This requires attentiveness to others as well as to Scripture.

(b)   *How can we find words which will carry weight because they arise out of the interaction between Scripture and life?*

We know that words are only approximate to experience, but they need to be authentic, because true in our experience and accessible to those we address. How do we arrive at such words?

We tackle the first question by examining the cultures around us, looking for possible entry points of Gospel interpretation. In Chapter 5 we move to the second. We recognise that we cannot produce answers for every situation.

11   Individual Christians are less likely to find answers if they fail to seek the help of others. We all read Scripture with lenses that give us a view on life that is particular, limited and sometimes distorted. We therefore need to correct and widen our perceptions by interacting with Christians of the past and the present who have lived, or are living, in other cultures and realities. The contribution of others in the World Church, their local theologies, their action in society, their priorities for the Church can be extremely valuable here. It is often said that we are 'insular' and not part of the Anglican Communion. It is hoped that the closer integration of the voluntary Missionary Societies with our new

Board of Mission will enable those with experience of the World Church more easily to feed in the pertinent insights. An adequate theology of the Church and revelation are also part of this process and a knowledge of church history can help us avoid blind alleys and galloping simplifications.

12   Above all we need the conviction that God wants to show us himself and the way we should go. He gives the promised Holy Spirit 'to lead us', in company with our fellow Christians, 'into all truth'. The knowledge of God's will comes not only from seeking it with mind and heart but from willingness to do it. 'He who does the will of God will know whether my teaching comes from him' (Jn 7.17). We can get so complicated and nervous in our seeking of God's will that we never *do* anything. The best model is surely to consider the situation, bring it to God with prayer and Bible, choose from among the possible courses of action, give one a try and bring the result back for reflection and prayer. In this way we can become 'living Bibles'.

Chapter 2

THE CHURCH AND CONTEMPORARY SOCIETY

Culture affects us all
13   If we are to 'look for what God is trying to say to us in our particular contemporary situation' the first point to be made is that for all people their 'particular contemporary situation' will include not only the *individual* circumstances in which they find themselves but also their *general cultural* background. Every Christian in Britain lives in a secular culture and in one or more of its various sub-cultures. The second point to be made is that the individual cultural background of most readers of this Report will itself be 'churchy'. It is only too easy for church members, particularly those belonging to flourishing congregations, to forget the fact that a particular church culture is not universal.

14   How people combine the influences of these various sub-cultures is the very stuff of this Report. Some Christians will be deeply involved in their 'church culture', giving a lot of their time in church activities and fellowship. Others will perhaps only worship in church on Sundays and in the week be more involved within their 'secular' contexts. A careful look at 'secularisation' and the various sub-cultures may help towards an understanding both of what God is doing in them and how Christians can find effective ways of speaking of God's activity within them. We must, however, begin by recognising the gap between Church and contemporary society.

Church culture and general western culture
15   Anthropologists find it far from easy to make a clear distinction between culture and religion. Members of the Church of England have equally found it difficult to make a clear distinction between western culture and the Christian way of life. As is well known, nineteenth-century missionaries were examples of devotion and sacrifice, often facing disease and death in order to share the Gospel in Africa, Asia and Latin America and bringing the blessings of education and medicine. At the same time they exported a church life that reflected a mixture of the Christian Gospel and western culture. Although some

of them (e.g. those working amongst the Tamils) had a deep respect for indigenous culture, the majority used entirely western models. They introduced organs and used western hymns. They put up buildings that were replicas of parish churches in Britain. They expected African brides to wear white and be given wedding rings. They rejected all forms of polygamy out of hand. They also exported certain assumptions about authority, styles of leadership and ownership of land and resources.

16 The same process can be detected *within* Britain. It is often claimed that the Church of England has failed to reach the working classes because it is bound to a suburban or middle class culture, and, further, that it has produced its own special ecclesiastical culture. Unfortunately it seems that only those who have once known some form of this culture (e.g. as children) are likely to rejoin a church as adults. We could wish there was more evidence of direct adult conversion from the growing majority of people who have never learnt the cultic language and ritual of the Church. After all, Christianity is not dependent on one cultural expression of it.

The question of language
17 Language is an important reflection of culture and is therefore particularly relevant to the life of the Church. People in Latin America speak about the 'torture and execution' of Jesus Christ rather than about his crucifixion, because that ties in with their own experience of life and struggle. More often, however, proclamation of the Gospel seems to be imprisoned in special 'cultic' language. Even some modern hymns in Britain are full of old religious phrases endlessly re-cycled. Such a perpetuation of tradition can be justified only if language generally has stood still (which it hardly ever does), if people's experience of life has not developed in any way (which it almost certainly will have done), and if the language still being used was entirely appropriate in the first place (which it may well not have been).

> There was a rich mush with kushti-disking purple togs. By his jigger suttied a poor mush called Lazarus.

18 The problem is partly illustrated through the process of translation from one language to another. It is not only a question of finding the

word in one language which will most accurately reproduce the meaning of the word in the original. It is also a question of creating the right 'impression' in the mind of the reader. Which is the more effective recreation of the Greek original – 'My soul doth magnify the Lord' or 'Tell out, my soul, the greatness of the Lord'? But that question in fact makes little sense as it stands. One must amplify it by saying 'effective *for whom*'? The quotation printed at the foot of page 11 may communicate effectively with members of the Romany community in this country. Does it do the same for members of the Afro-Caribbean communities? The opening words of the *Magnificat* may stir appropriate associations in the hearts and minds of members of the average Evensong congregation, but what do they say (in *either* version) to those millions of our fellow citizens who have never been to Evensong in their lives?

How 'normal' is church life?
19   The problem confronting us, however, is not confined simply to questions about language. It also has to do with patterns of thought and behaviour, and areas of concern. New arrivals at church are asked to do things which can seem very strange to them. They are also very often asked *not* to do things which seem quite normal to those outside the fellowship. How often, for example, does one find anything like the following sentence in a parish church's Notices?

> The Festival Mass always ends with a bar and steel bands in the crypt rounded off by a spectacular firework display from the steeple.

20   To the outsider people in church also *appear to think in a funny way*. The focus of their thoughts always seems to be in the past. They are always using concepts which do not seem to be rooted in everyday experience. This makes them appear not merely 'odd' but largely *irrelevant*. The real concerns which the average person has to carry through the day do not seem to surface in what the Church gets up to in its weekly pattern of meetings and services.

21   It is perfectly true that the Gospel can itself be a 'cause of offence' to individuals confronted and challenged by it. This is quite a different matter, however, from the Church allowing itself to become either an

offence to people, or an irrelevance in their eyes, simply because it fails to grasp the size and nature of the cultural gap which distances it from the vast majority of the citizens of this country. It would in fact be better to speak of 'cultural gaps' in the plural, because Britain today is a highly complex society containing a variety of different sub-cultures, indeed a variety of different cultures, in its midst. These 'gaps' constitute barriers to the transmission of the Gospel. If we are to overcome them, the first question we must ask is - What are the *entry points* into these other cultures? The next chapter explores a number (but by no means all) of the cultural layers in contemporary Britain and suggests possible points of contact between these cultures and the Gospel we are seeking to communicate.

Chapter 3

OUR SECULAR CULTURE AND SOME OF ITS SUB-CULTURES

The growth of secularisation

Why is the Church marginalised?
22 It is often said that Britain and the rest of Europe are post-Christian, secular societies. With the exception of some Pentecostal, ethnic and house churches (all of which tend to see themselves as being 'set apart' from the rest of society) there has been an overall decline in church-going, dating apparently from about 1920, i.e. the end of the First World War. Yet recent surveys in a number of European countries claim that 70% of the population say that they believe in God and pray. To be religious is of course not necessarily to be Christian, but even among those who claim to be Christian there are many who rarely attend a church. They may define a Christian as someone who lives a good moral life or as someone who holds to a form of belief about Jesus Christ. For many the figure of Jesus is attractive, but the Church is not.

A survey of religious belief among 11-16 year olds undertaken by Gallup in August 1990, revealed that 59% believed in God, as opposed to 24% who did not. 8% believed intermittently while 9% did not know.

Why is western culture secularised?
23 People from other cultures, like those found in most parts of Africa, Latin America and Asia, find our culture very irreligious. In their countries religion is taken for granted and in some of them Churches flourish and grow. Why is our culture so secularised? Three contemporary writers offer some pointers.

The Post-Enlightenment theory

24 Bishop Lesslie Newbigin,[1] among others, argues that secularisation arises partly from the intellectual assumptions of the movements of thought generally called the Enlightenment. Enlightenment culture radically divides 'the public world of scientific facts' from 'the private world of moral and religious opinions'. 'Facts' can be objectively known and must be accepted as undisputed reality, irrespective of a person's religious beliefs or moral convictions. 'Opinions' are subjective, personal and relative; they are purely a matter of individual choice. As a result, science and technology control public life, whereas religious doctrines and ethical commitments belong to the private sphere of interpretation and cannot be proclaimed as truths which compel a particular belief.

25 According to this view of Enlightenment assumptions religious commitment could lead in any one of numerous directions, depending on the cultural background, upbringing or personal inclinations of each individual. Paganism and secularism are equally valid choices. This rigid divorce between the natural world, which we must accept as given and in principle totally comprehensible, and the ethical and spiritual world, where one is free to believe and act as one wants, is the central characteristic of modern western society. Addressing and challenging this generally accepted conviction of our culture must be the central part of any new evangelisation of western societies and peoples.

Contemporary modifications

26 Newbigin notes, however, that in recent scientific discussions the earlier contrast between 'fact' and 'value' has been modified. Scientists are now acknowledging that their theories have to begin with a number of hypotheses, which are not themselves open to the process of scientific verification. They rest ultimately on a stand of 'faith'. For example, it is now recognised that absolute objectivity is not possible. We cannot avoid *interpreting* what we see, even when we try to make allowances for the values we acknowledge we hold. When we attempt to examine an object or situation, what we see and then report is affected not only by our very presence in the situation but also by our prior beliefs and prejudices. So a perspective on the world in which faith and reason have to be integrated is increasingly common in scientific circles. Recognition of what actually happens in the process of scientific investigation refutes the popular division of life into publicly acknowledged facts and privately held values and beliefs. The indispensable

need for an integrated view of the world makes a genuine dialogue between the Gospel and modern culture possible once again.

Wolfhart Pannenberg's explanation
27 The German theologian, Wolfhart Pannenberg,[2] brings a different perspective and additional insights to the question. The shift, he says, is not first from God to non-belief, but from a church-dominated society to a society of free choice. The roots of the religious decline he traces to the religious wars of the sixteenth and seventeenth centuries. People rebelled against imposed religion and religious intolerance. The non-conformist conscience was born and then the right of free choice between a particular religious adherence or none. People feel free to reflect what they perceive the Churches to be offering.

28 Going with this, there grew the view that human reason did not need a God to believe in. As scientific discoveries seemed to give totally adequate explanations of increasingly large areas of life, and as the technological advances flowing from the sciences brought ever more aspects of life under rational human domination, so the intellectual and practical need for God became less and less evident. If today there still remain mysterious parts of life, or circumstances which cannot be controlled by normal means, most people fall back on popular religious notions and practices or turn to semi-magical beliefs to help them to cope. The God of the historic Christian faith is not perceived to be central to most of life's concerns. Freed from the authority of the Church, there is no need to believe in him.

Peter Berger and the necessity of choice
29 Taking these ideas even further Peter Berger,[3] the American socio-logist, has emphasised that because of the development of technology the prime characteristic of a modern society is not only the possibility but the *necessity* of choice. The acceptance of authority in a free society – whether political, religious or moral – is also a matter of choice. Choice is particularly enhanced as a result of technological develop-ments in communication. People are able to choose from an international supermarket of *ideas* as well as of material goods, and the process of 'secularisation' stems from their insistence on exercising that choice.

> The term 'secularisation' (freedom from
> ecclesiastical control) must be distinguished
> from the term 'secularism' (the belief that no
> part of life can be related to a divine being).

30 Christians will of course reject secularism, but are bound to admit that western culture, even though far from being fully secular, is now fully secularised. They may indeed celebrate the freedom which secularised society offers for choice, for God gives us freedom to choose, and right choice is a way to maturity. Unfortunately we all suffer from wrong choices; this is why the Gospel speaks of God's forgiveness and his enabling

The extent of secularisation
31 It is not only in matters of religious belief that people are now exercising their own choices. The same is true in relation to moral values. Nearly every aspect of contemporary western society is affected by secularisation – attitudes to marriage and family life, economic and political goals, approaches to education, the self-understanding of young people.

> **The British Social Attitudes Survey,** 1990
> Among those aged 55+, 63% disapproved,
> among those aged 17-34, 83% positively
> approved of prospective partners living
> together before marriage.

Marriage in our secularised society
32 If we examine attitudes to marriage and family life, we find that even though there is little evidence to suggest that cohabitation is totally replacing marriage, living together without formal marriage is becoming much more common. The prospect of children may lead people to marry but this is not necessarily the case. In 1989, 27% of all births occurred outside marriage. However, two-thirds of those were registered by both parents, which suggests that those children were born within stable unions, even though their parents were not legally married. [Charts 2.22, 2.24 *Social Trends* 21, HMSO 1991]

33   Nevertheless the majority of people still see the married state as a desirable one. In spite of a six-fold increase in the rate of divorce during the last twenty years, two-thirds of all marriages are ended by the death of one partner rather than by divorce. The increase in divorce has led, however, to a rise in the number of single parent families. It was estimated in 1987 that 14% of families in Britain were headed by a single parent, usually a woman. [Chart 2.8 *Social Trends* 21, HMSO 1991]

The Church's response
34   This pattern of changing relationships and changing attitudes to relationships presents particular challenges to the Christian church. The secular attitude to divorce suggests that most people see it as a legitimate liberation from an intolerable relationship. The institutional churches, however, seeking to uphold the ideal of marriage presented in the teaching of Jesus, often appear unsympathetic to failed marriages and remarriage. Divorce seems to be reluctantly accepted while remarriage may not be allowed in church. In fact Christians both uphold an ideal and work with the saving God to make the best of every human situation. The preacher and the pastor, the idealist and the pragmatist in all of us may get into conflict with each other and so prevent the Gospel of the just and saving God being heard.

35   This change in attitude and relationships calls into question some of the imagery we use in communicating the Gospel. The traditional Christian imagery relies on the experience of strong family relationships, particularly those centring on the father, and may make little impact on those whose family experiences have been so very different.

Affluent/enterprise cultures

Choice, but who for?
36   Peter Berger may well be right in suggesting that 'the prime characteristic of a modern society is the possibility of choice' but it must not be forgotten that choice is at any time open only to those with adequate resources. The poor man surrounded by a wealth of goods 'from which to choose' has in practice hardly any choice at all. People are also discovering that there are other restraints upon choice even in the midst of affluence.

37   Many individuals feel trapped by the present culture, though in very different ways. At the one end of the economic spectrum, 'the rat race' is a familiar description of what looks to others like success; at the

other is an acute awareness that the decisions are all taken by 'them' and 'we' are the ones who suffer. The two sub-cultures often live cheek by jowl in places like East London, where 'gentrification' has been speeded up by the Dockland Development enterprise. That both groups feel they have no real control over their own lives suggests a major entry point for the Gospel. The discovery that there is a sovereign God to whom all human beings are equally valuable and that the 'theys' (whoever they are) are finite, fallible and temporary brings new perspectives. The further recognition that God is involved in the world and suffers from 'man's inhumanity to man', that God's energy is at work to redeem and recreate and that he invites human beings to work with him is good news indeed.

38 Those in responsible jobs are nearly always aware of strain. The pressure of work, high speed, rapid technology and information saturation lead many towards 'burn out' comparatively young. At the other end of the spectrum frustration, boredom, the sense of being valueless, even unemployable, result in apathy or a negativity which may seek consolation in narcotics or else break out in destructive violence. Even where clear self-knowledge is possible, the recognition of the flaw in us and in others which produces guilt and a sense of failure is *bad* news. It can become good news only when God's acceptance of us in Jesus Christ is recognised as the starting-point for change.

Green culture

Concern for the future of the planet
39 As the affluent/enterprise culture, with its emphasis on initiative and choice, has grown throughout the last two decades, so there has also developed a 'green culture' which emphasises restraint and conservation. The spur for this has been the growing concern about seemingly irreversible damage to the future of the planet, which could threaten the future existence of human life. There are three main strands to this: damage to the ozone layer, global warming, which could affect food supplies and result in inundation of some land areas, and the large-scale destruction of the tropical rain forests.

40 There have been several responses to these problems. Many people, in order to limit damage, have changed their patterns of consumption. There has, for example, been a massive swing towards using 'ozone friendly' products. A lesser but still significant response has been made towards the conversion of cars to run on lead-free petrol. The idea of

abandoning private transport altogether would be adopted only if the environmental damage became markedly more obvious and was posing a greater, tangible threat.

41 As in all cultures, there are extremes. The limited changes in consumption are at one end of the spectrum. At the other are those who take the view that human beings cannot claim any special status in relation to the rest of the natural world. They would also give nature a quasi-mystical, intrinsic worth, a view typical of those caught up with New Age philosophies.

42 The Christian basis for active responsibility for the whole created earth rests on the concept of stewardship, the conviction that God holds human beings accountable for the way they treat the natural world, which he has entrusted to them as a gift. They have been given a commission by the Creator to respect, look after and use for the good of all the resources he has made. This view differs from some current beliefs about the unity of human beings with nature. For example among some who expound a 'New Age' philosophy '"Planet Earth" is the Mother Goddess, the great life-giver, the formant Power who is waiting for us all to be reconciled to *her* so that, attuned to her energies and rhythms, she will release her powers to lead us to the goal of evolution: reconciliation between humanity and her'.[4] For the Christian reconciliation with God, who has made all things, is of first importance. This entails a right relationship with the earth, including a just and restrained exploiting of its resources. For New Age thinking unity with nature, which is the origin of our being, *is* the healing process, at the deepest level, that we all need.

Urban priority areas

Feeling powerless
43 As we have noted, powerlessness is a common experience in our complex modern society. Everything always seems to be decided somewhere else. It is therefore important in all areas that the Church encourages as many people as possible to participate in decision-making. But this is particularly important in Urban Priority Areas where so many have become dependent through social pressures. Those who are not asked to make decisions at work or elsewhere in their lives are slow to do so in church.

44 In Western Parliamentary democracy we are used to debate and confrontation. The General Synod accepts this cultural pattern, modelled as it is on Parliament. But in many Asian cultures, for example, there is a deliberate avoidance of confrontation. If a decision were reached simply by a majority vote the minority would suffer 'loss of face'. Seeking consensus is therefore the approach used. There are parallels in UPA cultures. An incumbent from the North East comments, 'Whether a decision sticks depends on whether the process is conducted properly. People may not articulate objections at the meeting but will go away without "owning" the decision and nothing will happen'. Behind this approach is a concern to affirm those who lack a sense of their own value and who felt themselves to be failures at school.

Alienated from the Church
45 In contrast to many other parts of the world, the Church in this country has rarely seen the poorer sectors of the community within its ranks. Perhaps the majority of them would not even bring their children for baptism, let alone attend other church services. The most obvious reason why people from a deprived background do not form part of the Church is because they do not feel they belong. For them everything about the Church – its professionalised leadership, its liturgical life, its way of organising itself – smacks of another world, one which appears wholly unfamiliar and unattractive. Those who do attend seem part of another culture. They are financially secure, able to lead a mobile and varied life, relatively articulate and used to handling books. One old lady at a Coventry church said as she was handed her pile of modern service books, 'When you come to this church you need a Sainsbury's trolley'.

A non-literary culture
46 Relative affluence is not the only distinguishing feature of the professional classes in a modern society. Theirs is a sub-culture characterised by intellectual, rational and academic approaches to the problems confronting them. The written word is their chief form of communication. Such intellectual devices are not employed by the majority in this country. This is a crucial point to emphasise in a report such as this, which uses precisely those techniques which are inappropriate for most people. The following example illustrates the point.

47 About 20 adults are in a church hall for an educational evening, but none of them has paper, pencil or pen. Only the leader has a marker pen and he uses it occasionally to draw a picture or a diagram. They

are talking about the issues which are important to their local community, and deciding what to do about them. Perhaps what is even more important, they are discussing *why* it is important to make sure something satisfactory is done. The title of this programme is *People Who Can Read But Don't* and it is organised by the Evangelical Urban Training Project (EUTP).[5] The Project is based in Liverpool, but offers consultancy help to churches and other organisations all over the country. It recognises that whereas most people in this country *can* read, books and other literature have not become part of the culture of most. They find it more acceptable to take in information pictorially, whether through television or comics.

That is why Jim Hart, the EUTP officer, only allows the leader to have pencils and paper. The group learns to discuss and reflect on the issues which affect them at home, at work, in unemployment. They discuss and plan to do something about what is immediately important. Afterwards they will talk through what they have learned from the experience – it may be practical skills or principles to guide future action.

48 The alien nature of the Christian Church and the perceived superiority of those who belong to it have erected for the gospel message an immense barrier before the hearts and minds of deprived individuals and communities. It poses certainly one of the greatest challenges to Christians who are committed to serving the one who revealed himself supremely as the friend of the outsider. We can, however, take encouragement from the experiences recorded in *Living Faith in the City*, which offers many examples of how the Good News of Christ can be effectively heard in the inner city and other Urban Priority Areas.

Youth culture

The world their oyster?

49 Young people in Britain today, just as much as adults, are faced with a constant series of choices. They make regular and daily choices about what to do with their money, what music to listen to, what to wear, who they want to go out with, what kind of sexual life they want. They are taught that making choices is 'what life's all about' and therefore the wider the choice available the better for everyone. Indeed, the breadth of choice so clearly available to this generation is much wider that it ever has been before and is becoming increasingly wider. This is true not only of fashion, of food or of music. As new drinks have come on the market, so have new drugs, and they have become more

readily available. For many there is a real option now to travel and even to live and work abroad, especially within the European Community.

50 Yet at the same time as society offers this wide range of choices, many young people are left unable to take advantage of them. This may be true of young people possibly to an even greater extent than it is of their parents. Because of poor educational provision, especially in the tougher areas of our inner cities, many leave school ill-equipped and under-qualified for the high-technology job market. Young people growing up emotionally starved by their parents, or bullied at school, find it difficult to choose anything other than the quick excitement of easy sex and a good night out. Financial deprivation and a future that seems to offer little sends many young men and women off down the spiral of drug abuse, sexual aggression and crime. As one young man from the Home Counties said, 'I see the white kids who went to the snobby school making really good money, buying houses and driving smart cars, and I think to myself "If only I'd been made to study". As it is, the only way for a black man in this town to live a quality life is crime.'

Religion among the young
51 To what extent will these young people's choices be affected by anything they may have acquired from 'the religious heritage' of the country? The answer is probably: hardly at all. Unless young people are from church-going families, then they are likely to have picked up little that has stuck from state religious education, if indeed they have received any at all. They may have picked up some stories while at primary school, but as they grow older, RE will in many cases have been replaced by general moral education or social skills. Contact with the Church will have been limited most probably to baptisms, marriages and funerals, which has also been the limited experience of their parents. And so nothing can be assumed by way of knowledge or understanding of the Christian faith.

52 In one sense, therefore, we cannot over-estimate the loss of religious consciousness and knowledge in young people, yet in another sense we should not underestimate an innate feeling for the spiritual in general. The world of the imagination in childhood is still alive; the popularity of the C.S. Lewis' *Narnia* stories on television went beyond the childhood age. The occult, and films and literature connected with it, are popular with youth. These latter contain danger, but even this

material seems to answer a desire to reach beyond the world of here and now and the empirical realities of modern life.

53   Young people have concerns with which church people will not be comfortable. Perhaps foremost amongst these will be their personal relationships, heterosexual and homosexual; they face the reality of AIDS and grow up under its shadow. Their concerns may include those once so easily dismissed by their seniors as youthful idealism, like green issues, vegetarianism, animal rights, concern about nuclear war, apartheid in South Africa and racism in this country. Some young people may be concerned with none of these things, and only themselves; but in this way they mirror much that current society appears to encourage anyway.

Teenage crises
54   Teenage years have always been times of crisis, but perhaps now more than ever before. Young people may be subject to the pressure to leave home even though there is nowhere stable to go; family break-ups, unwanted pregnancies, abortions, and the anguish over never-to-be-born children all contribute. There may be the hopelessness of being unemployed and unwanted, in an increasingly affluent and status conscious society. How are we to show that our Gospel is really good news in such circumstances?

55   Many young people face funerals, terminal illness, and family traumas very early in their life. The public face of the Church needs to be visible at these moments of crisis. The hospital bed and the crematorium, though vital places for the urgency and relevance of faith to be conveyed, need to be supplemented by the youth club, the school, the pub. How often, if a regular punter at the local pub died, would the vicar visit the pub, to say a prayer, to listen to emotions, to keep silence with those left behind? In a parish in Coventry the hostility between a local predominantly black youth club and the church was felt to disappear overnight when the curate chose, on the death of a 19 year old member of the club, to go along on club night and lead five minutes' silence and the singing of a couple of hymns.

Bridging the cultural gap
56   We must not, however, ignore the fact that from church congregations, school Christian Unions, church-linked youth organisations and a variety of other sources, impressive young Christians are emerging.

They may have a deep experience of Christ, an informal and questioning mind about Christian truth, a warm sense of Christian fellowship and an awareness of the vast needs and opportunities in the contemporary world. Many such young people give a year or more voluntary service at home or abroad. They all bring enthusiasm, hope and encouragement to other Christians and live a wholesome full-blown Christian life which many older Christians may envy. All the agencies which enable such Christians to emerge need congratulation and encouragement. If we say that such young people belong to a Christian sub-culture that is not to say that they are out of touch with the aspirations and needs of their contemporaries.

57 Nevertheless, youth workers rightly emphasise that the vast majority of the young people they encounter on the streets have a quite different experience of life from most of those young people who are in the churches. A Youth for Christ worker in Coventry, for example, found the way forward was to organise an evening fellowship group in an alcohol-free bar, and talk of Jesus and the Gospel simply and directly. Part of the evening was social, when young people could speak about what they wished. During the rest of the evening he enabled them to make their own worship, prayer and sermon. They wrote simple prayers and songs, and drew cartoons which they explained; the group shared stories, and maybe acted one out. And everything was done in their vocabulary. Only slowly was the Bible introduced. The young people were the creators, and not just the audience.

58 We need to think much more about worship as happening outside the confines of 'normal' Church services. The experiments in Sheffield, where an alternative-culture event happens for young people every Sunday evening at 9, with excellent music, proper lighting and a social atmosphere, may not seem much like worship to many of us, but may be the way ahead. There can be a real sense of spiritual longing expressed even in much of the erotic music of today. However unlikely it may seem, here too is a possible entry point for the Gospel.

Other ethnic cultures

Afro-Caribbean culture

59 Even a limited review of the cultural scene in Britain today must include some consideration of those communities whose ethnic origins are from abroad. The story of Afro-Caribbean immigration raises par-

ticular questions, not least because of the history of European colonialisation in Africa and the Caribbean; this highlights many of the issues
raised by the interaction of Gospel and Culture. While Afro-Caribbean
peoples share a common historical experience and so have a common
culture, they exhibit a rich variety of religious experience. Many who
had been nurtured in the main-stream churches in the Caribbean suffered a trauma when they felt rejected by the main-stream churches in
the Mother Country. The middle-class bias and blatant racism they
encountered caused them to turn their backs on these churches. Some
have become impervious to the Gospel, while others have turned
towards the black-led churches. However, many blacks have retained
membership of main-stream churches, but have not yet achieved the
position of exercising leadership and of being part of the decision-making structures. The continuing class bias and racism within the church
have been well documented.[6] Before proclaiming that it is properly
equipped to preach the Gospel the Church needs to take to heart the maxim
'Tell me what the Church *does* and I'll tell you what it believes.'

60   The Caribbean has been a melting-pot of many cultures. The dominant European culture was transplanted to this area and the African
culture was submerged, but not obliterated, in the demonic institution
of human slavery. The established church was part and parcel of the
colonial superstructure, so the process of evangelisation and civilisation
(European) were one and the same process, although some of the
land-owners were ambivalent about the evangelisation of the blacks,
in case they experienced a sense of equality and fostered agitation about
liberation. Others, on the other hand, felt the Gospel might engender a
spirit of obedience, humility and diligence.

61   With emphasis by the established church on baptism, monogamous
marriage, family life and sabbath observance, features of African culture remained submerged. With the abolition of slavery and its
aftermath the dominant European culture was still the cradle of the
Gospel. But gradually African features, which had been submerged,
surfaced and in this century have made their distinctive contribution
to Afro-Caribbean culture. The result is a culture where the two worlds
of Europe and Africa meet. The influence of the established church and
non-conformist churches is still to be seen, but so is that of the Afro-
Caribbean cults with their conflation of African and Christian religious
customs and rituals, along with the growth of Pentecostalism and
Rastafarianism.

62 A significant feature of British religious life is the phenomenal growth of the black-led churches. While some Afro-Caribbean people brought these traditions with them, others have adopted them since arriving here because of rejection by the main-stream churches. Whatever the reasons, there has been a creative interaction between gospel and Afro-Caribbean culture, as persons hear the Word of God in their context, express their art-forms in worship, and experience a sense of belonging to a caring and supportive community, with leadership emerging from among their own religious communities.

Asian culture
63 With the Asian communities the situation is somewhat different. Christianity has never permeated any Asian culture to the extent that it has the Afro-Caribbean. There is therefore no one simple approach to these communities, and we have sought case study material to illustrate the various ways that a response can be made. In one church, where the evangelistic imperative is paramount in all that church's work, a considerable number of Asians of various religious origins have become Christians. Some have come into the Church with their families, some as individuals. They are part of the main church body, but naturally the 'feel' in that body is that of a traditional English evangelical church. It is therefore the Asian young people who have been best able to fit in with the church structures, sharing as they do common schooling with the other young members of the church. For most adults what has been crucial has been a Sunday afternoon Asian Christian Fellowship, and mid-week Bible study groups, where Asian languages and forms of worship indigenous to their culture can be used. There is also Asian paid leadership in the parish, though not ordained as yet. This is leadership not only in worship, pastoral ministry and evangelism, but in an impressive outreach to the social needs of the Asian community in the area.

64 A somewhat similar story concerns a devout Sikh.
A first generation immigrant and her husband were converted to Christianity and became keen evangelical Christians. Around them grew up a group of some 30 new Christians from similar Asian backgrounds. They worshipped on Sunday afternoons in a local church hall, led in their Holy Communion service by the Vicar who had worked overseas. The older folk loved the singing accompanied by Asian musical instruments, while the younger folk favoured guitars. Both Punjabi and English were used in their worship. Some of them went also to the morning English service and two were elected to the PCC.

Most, however, kept to the margins. Members of the Asian congregation differed amongst themselves about Asian customs, dress and conventions. The Vicar hopes eventually to integrate the two congregations but recognises the difficulty of Punjabi prayers for an English congregation and the value of maintaining a group in which the Asians feel at home.

Cross-cultural stress

65 The cultural stresses felt by converts should not be underestimated. The Church needs to recognise how difficult it usually is to cross a cultural boundary. As well as giving practical help to converts in overcoming this problem, Christians must learn their own lessons from this situation. In looking at our secular culture with its diverse sub-cultures we have looked also for points of entry for the Gospel and the Church. We should recognise, however, that following up those points of entry will involve its own form of crossing cultural boundaries. In our current situation we need to encourage one another to take initiatives and risks, sensitively but openly, in approaching those around us who differ from us by opinion or culture. One prayer for the Decade of Evangelism reads: 'Set us free, O God to cross barriers for you, as you crossed barriers for us in Jesus Christ, our Lord'.[7]

Chapter 4

BUILDING BRIDGES FOR TWO-WAY TRAFFIC

Crossing cultural boundaries

66 Christians have many deeply-valued treasures which they long to share. The attempt to express the Gospel in the terms of Western secularised culture has engaged theologians throughout the century. Christians in their daily lives likewise seek, or are presented with, opportunities to communicate the Good News. They may find it difficult to translate what they have received in one idiom, (e.g. Scripture or liturgy) into the idiom of contemporary life and thought. As well as language, communication is a matter of relationship between people: exchange can only happen where there is real meeting. Bridges enable traffic both ways.

67 The Church as a whole has come to recognise the need to avoid any notion that the Gospel is a bundle of concepts which by skilful packaging and good marketing can be taken on by all people irrespective of individual circumstance. Unfortunately this recognition has tended to move the Church from what might have been a noisy irrelevance to what is seen as a sad silence. The Decade of Evangelism provides a good stimulus to discovering what the Gospel is for different people in the here and now. If it can be discovered again in a way that truly communicates it could spread like a forest fire. What follows here is a beginning, just one attempt to explore formulations of the Gospel which speak directly to the needs and circumstances of many of our contemporaries in the secularised, enterprise culture that characterises Britain today.

A religion-shaped gap?

68 The absence of adequate religious education and of accepted channels of religious expression leaves many individuals today with an inner vacuum, especially those living in greatly weakened social and moral structures. New Religious Movements aim to fill the vacuum by combining idealism with apparent certitude. Varieties of Eastern religions from Buddhism (which offers discipline and meditation but does

not require any belief in God) to inclusive groups like Baha'i (which recognise all religions as paths to God) meet the need for some. Perhaps most people, however, settle for trying to enjoy what life deals out for them and hope that God will be kind. The experience of loving and being loved in friendship, sex, and family, the absence of major anxiety about food and basics, some opportunity of being with others, working at something and being able to give, the consolations of leisure, recreation, television, a garden, neighbourliness, belonging, association with others, a chance to travel, a sense of freedom, these are life's daily components and compensations for many. A minority looks for fulfilment in working for change through a political party, an issue-based group, an ideology, a cause or the like. Some in malfunction or dissatisfaction look to psychotherapy or the many 'human potential' movements to find help and growth. For others, again, life can only be experienced and endured as disappointment, frustration, resentment, oppression, bitterness and near despair.

69   Christians are themselves to be found in many of these categories, and share many of these experiences. Christian fellowship, in its many manifestations, meets some of the same needs as other groups. It is not that Christians have to learn a completely new way of looking at the world in order to communicate with those outside their fellowship, and yet many of those who formally represent the Christian message do it in a way which suggests that they have little understanding of those who find life a constant struggle. Perhaps such Christians are actually using their religion to mask their own problem in coping with such struggles.

A world apart?
70   Within this context the Church of England is seen as being, in the worst sense of the term, 'in a class of its own'. To many it seems to have become just another option, a lifestyle which attracts only a limited few. It seems to cater in the main for a very traditional taste in music. It relies on the written and spoken word rather than visual images, on the intellectual rather than the emotional. When there is outreach, it tends to presume that 'They will come to us'. Christian maturity is often portrayed as getting to like church pretty much as it is, with little accommodation to things that are new. If we are really doing no more than asking people to opt into a Church culture, and out of their own, then we are almost certain to fail in the endeavour. It is arguable that the discovery of a new readiness on the part of Christians to acknow-

ledge openly that they too are deeply affected by modern culture, that they are *not* different from those around them, is crucial to the evangelistic task today.

71 This is by no means the same as saying that Christians have no message that they can bring to the secularised world of which they are in fact so fully a part. Where they *do* differ from their fellow-citizens is that they bring a different perspective to what is otherwise a shared experience of the world. Christian hope abounds in models and images of a new society supported by the conviction that God will bring humanity to the realisation of its potential. The sense of adventure and discovery which arises from this faith is energising and refreshing. The purposelessness which characterises so much of modern society (cf. 37 above) can, in this context, give way to a real sense of purposefulness.

'Where love is....'?

72 In all the above discoveries there is the Christian good news of what it means to be human. The increasing use of hi-tech instruments and the emergence of forces which operate independently of individual choice militate against human development. Further if the strain of such work leads people to seek relief in escapes or self-centred pleasures, the experience of loving and being loved may be driven to the periphery of human experience whereas in God's purposes it is at the heart of the whole human being. Christians affirm a God whose very nature is interdependent love. This love has been demonstrated in the whole life of Jesus, who has shown us exactly what God is like, and is made available to all who desire to be transformed into the image of Jesus, by the Spirit who creates communities of self-giving, loving concern. This affirmation about God cleanses and reinforces the quest for a restored humanity and grounds it in God's purposes.

73 Some Christians would deny any spiritual value outside the context of explicit faith in Christ. It is, of course, a simple fact that the spiritual lives of many people in our present-day secular culture are so far distanced from what happens in churches that it is difficult for *anyone* (whether inside or outside the church) to recognise these experiences as being in any way religious. Yet as Sir Alister Hardy,[8] amongst others, has reminded us people do have values, loves, glimpses of reality, moral assumptions and imperatives. There is need for both groups, those outside the church and those within, to recognise God in one another's experiences. This follows from the conviction that

God has not left himself without a witness and that all things are created in and for Christ. The Spirit also is working in people's consciences to bring a conviction of right and wrong, of moral accountability and of the hope of a better world. Dialogue with people who have no personal knowledge of God in Christ can nonetheless reveal the marks of his presence in their lives. This can occur with those on the fringes of the Church (e.g. those who, for purely conventional reasons, present their children for baptism), with those from other faiths, or with those entirely outside *any* faith community.

74 We shall explore some of these situations in a little more detail but the need for Christians to think constantly in terms of 'building bridges' cannot be over-stressed. Perhaps those who have had most experience of this approach to sharing the good news of the Gospel are industrial, university and hospital chaplains, school teachers (especially RE specialists), intellectuals in universities and elsewhere, broadcasters and media Christians. But at a more ordinary level, Christians who take seriously the attitudes of people around them and try to relate them to Gospel values do have the opportunity of making positive links. Someone whose culture does not allow them to name God may acknowledge in a very developed way beauty, goodness, justice, compassion, moral responsibility for others, etc and may put their insights fully into practice. Christians who work with such people, perhaps on common human causes, will find plenty of opportunities of witness. Dr Elaine Storkey has found that involvement in feminist issues, for example, often means that she is working alongside many who have rejected the Christian Church or have never even had contact with it, yet 'when you really get to the deep centre of things, your deepest convictions will emerge, and for me that is God as experienced in the Christian faith'. Or again in inter-faith dialogue it will not be long before Christians will need to declare themselves about Jesus and to say 'Yes, we believe in a crucified God'. In all these instances it is the *two-way involvement* that provides the setting for Christian witness, and such sharing in dialogue can lead both non-Christians *and* Christians to new enriching experience.

Chapter 5

IDENTIFYING THE GOSPEL IN ACTION

Holding to the essentials

75 It is quite clear that the Church can never be culturally neutral. In one sense, as we have argued, a church needs to be fully open to the culture (or, rather, cultures) in the local community that it serves. In another sense it cannot avoid being a society with its own culture and language. In both these situations it is vital that it is constantly seeking to distinguish between what is cultural overlay and what are the essentials of the Gospel.

76 In practice Christians differ as to how far contemporary culture should be allowed to shape the way we speak the Gospel. Some say that unless the Church offers something which people from all our different cultures can perceive as good news, or unless it can share with people from those cultures in discerning what good news there is, the Church will become increasingly marginal and ignored. Some have hopes that we are in a new period of discovery, a transitional or 'hinge' period, where Christians along with others will discover a way of life beyond our present cultural norms. Others, however, fear that the 'cultural sensitivity' which their fellow-Christians are urging contains within itself a minimalising tendency and potential confusion about the boundary between the Gospel and culture which would prevent the Gospel having its proper impact on those very people who need it most.

Differing vantage-points?

77 There is no guarantee that any one group of Christians, rather than any other, can come to a sure understanding of particular aspects of God's self-revelation and its significance for today. However, it may well be true that some groups are more likely to capture the meaning of Jesus Christ than others, because of the vantage-point from which they are hearing about him. Thus, if Jesus Christ came preaching Good News to the poor, then the poor may well have an advantage both in understanding what the Gospel is about and in receiving it gladly. Likewise, those called upon to suffer for their faith, or those who have been

33

healed of physical or emotional disabilities by God's power are likely more readily to understand other passages of the Scriptures.

78   God's special concern for the poor, the need for the poor to evangelise the rich, and the Church's bias to the poor are all unfamiliar and unpalatable ideas for middle-class and affluent Christians. Many members of the Church of England, and especially those who attend Sunday worship, belong to the rich in this world in terms of standards of living and educational and cultural opportunities. They may find many Gospel sayings about riches difficult to reconcile with their style of life, and this may colour their 'understanding' of those passages. Equally they may be particularly aware of their need of help from God in sustaining them in their responsibilities and in the pressures and strains of their working life.

79   In both situations consciousness is raised about the challenge of the Good News, for others as well as for themselves. Good News must at the very least mean some form of liberation from oppression. In some parts of the world this may be as dramatic as the throwing off of a tyrannical regime. In others it may be an attempt to deal with the meaninglessness of life (whether under Spaghetti Junction or in Threadneedle Street) by providing people with information and advice that empowers them to take responsibility for improving their own lives.

The focus of the Gospel

> The focus of the Gospel is of course the story of the birth, death, resurrection and ascension of Jesus Christ.

80   God sent his only Son into the world to live out his love, so that we might live through him (1 Jn 4.9; cf Jn 20.19-23; Phil 2.5-11). God sent his Son to be the expiation for our sins (1 Jn 4.10). The Father sent his Son as Saviour of the world (1 Jn 4.14). Jesus has come so that we may have life (Jn 10.10).[9] But although the focus of the Gospel is indeed that story, the Gospel itself is not a single unchanging package that simply has to be unwrapped. Each community and every individual has to be helped to discover how the Gospel is good news for them, by linking

their story to his story. It is, as we have seen, partly a question of language. For example, even though we have identified it as part of 'the focus of the Gospel', the word 'expiation' cannot be said to be widely used in contemporary culture. One must ask therefore how that crucial concept can best be conveyed to those around us including, it must be said, many of those *within* the Church.

'Discerning God's word at work in the world'

81 There are many Christians who argue that some concepts, even some actual words, are so central to the Gospel message and the way of looking at life that flows from it that there can be no 'modern substitute' for them. The relation between Gospel and culture, however, operates at a deeper level than that of vocabulary, or even of concepts. The New Testament offers a Gospel of such richness of meaning that people of differing generations and cultures have discovered fresh and varying significance in it. Sharing the Gospel in the context of a different culture has been likened to a person taking a plant from the soil of his or her own culture and rooting it in the soil of another – after all the word 'horticulture' derives from precisely the same root as 'culture' itself. But while the distinction of plant and soil may be helpful in some circumstances, and always important in principle, it may give rise to the implication that it is easy to make that distinction. That of course is not true. The Gospel is no more a single unchanging entity that has simply to be transplanted than it is a single package that has to be unwrapped.

> The encounter between God's word and God's world in a particular and local situation is often called 'contextual theology'

82 This problem has led many contemporary evangelists to adopt a more radical approach. Their understanding of the Gospel leads them to argue that their first task, in the light of their understanding of the Gospel, is to listen and learn in order to discover where and how God is at work in another culture, or in their own. This process of 'prophetic' encounter between God's word and God's world in a particular and local situation' is often called 'contextual theology'. It is an approach that demands reflection, action, then further reflection. The activities of GUML in Liverpool (see para. 242) provide examples of just such an

attempt at 'contextualisation', through which the issues of the day are seen as the starting point for reflecting on what God is seen to be doing within a particular community.

83   A possible danger of this approach is that the criteria we use to discern where and how God is at work in the world may echo the beliefs and assumptions of a particular philosophy, ideology, way of life or social programme which do not conform to a view of human existence centred in Jesus Christ. We need, therefore, to be able to apply criteria that will help us discover which forms of contextualisation are authentic expressions of the Gospel. We believe that when one or more of the following events and convictions are present in a situation the working of the gospel may be observed. We are calling the 'Ten Signs of Authenticity' in the belief that in different ways they point us to the reality of God's continuing work in Jesus Christ. They may be used, with due care, as a kind of check-list to avoid an over-hasty identification of the Gospel of the Kingdom of God with human desires and wisdom and so help us to establish where a real understanding of God is breaking through into human endeavours.

84   Ten Signs of Authenticity

1. *The recognition that the entire created order is a gift of God* (Ps 24.1; 1 Cor 3.21b-23)
Everything, including human life, is a gift. Fundamental questions must therefore be raised, where injustice, the exploitation of the environment, or social neglect as a consequence of the profit motive, deny the sacred trust we should exercise for the benefit of all sections of society.

2. *The affirmation of the supreme values of justice and loving-kindness* (Is 58.6-7; Mt 23.23)
When these values are not treated as abstract entities but are embodied in a particular culture, they set forth the nature of God and reveal in action his care for and re-establishment of the vulnerable and weak members of a community.

3. *The acceptance of the fact that all human beings are to be accorded equality in dignity and worth* (Acts 10.34)
This equality rests upon their creation in the image of a personal God and it requires all relations of dependence or inferiority to be challenged.

4. *An awareness of the existence of evil and suffering in the world* (Gen 6.13; Heb 2.14-18)

This involves the recognition of the extent to which self-interest is prevalent throughout all strata of society resulting in the treatment of human beings as means to ends, as objects to be manipulated to one's own advantage. This evil denies true humanity, is disruptive not only of personal life but of community and is embodied in structures of violence. In the suffering which this inflicts God also suffers. On the cross he accepts ultimate responsibility for both the evil and the suffering it causes, bears the pain himself and brings healing to the afflicted.

5. *The experiencing of forgiveness and reconciliation* (Col 1.21-22; Mt 5.23-24)

The vicious circle of enmity, hatred, guilt, fear and self-righteousness is broken by God's work in Christ and replaced by a new relationship with himself and with one another.

6. *The fostering of hope in a transformed order of human life* (1 Pet 1.3)

This hope rests upon the resurrection of Jesus from corruption to incorruption. It contradicts all situations of despair, and rejects the idea that nothing can be changed.

7. *The entering upon a new way of being human* (2 Cor 5.17)

This new way, as it was revealed and embodied in Jesus, includes challenging oppressive legalism. It also includes befriending sinners and outcasts and restoring physical, mental, spiritual and social wholeness.

8. *The enjoyment of responsible freedom* (Gal 5.13)

This enjoyment is the fruit of liberation *from* the bondage of self-centredness and, at the same time, it derives from liberation *for* a life of self giving and the service of others. Power can then be exercised not over other people but in partnership with them and on their behalf.

9. *The creation of life in community* (Rom 12.5)

Because to be truly human is to be members of one another, there is to be brought into being and maintained a society within which the talents and resources of all are shared on a reciprocal basis.

10. *The celebration of the Good News* (Ps 145; Lk 15.22-24)
Wherever good news is received, there is celebration. Wherever there are high points in everyday life, there are occasions for gratitude. Authentic humanity is maintained, even amidst adverse circumstances that deny it, when a worshipping community learns to live in hope and with thanks on its lips.

Part B

The Impact of the Gospel on Society

Chapter 6

HOW THE GOSPEL HAS AFFECTED BRITISH CULTURE

Its impact through the structures of society
85 We must start with the word 'culture' itself. There is more than one definition of the word, and probably we have to admit that different definitions fit different circumstances. This does not always make for clarity of discussion. Culture is the compound of customs, priorities, values, assumptions and beliefs shared by a social group or community. Culture has to do with the cohesion of a society and with a sense of its identity. It stems in part from history. The great difficulty which the Church in the western world has in finding an effective voice springs paradoxically from the fact that Church and State, Gospel and Culture have been so closely intertwined in previous centuries. Today the achievements in society and culture expressed in the Christendom model of medieval society will be variously evaluated. For some it is still a great idea. Others view it as a great disaster. Either way the fact remains that with the breakup of Christendom and the rise of the nation state the creation of the Church of England provided a continuing sense of identity for the country as a whole and, despite many vagaries on the way, it has served that purpose, with varying degrees of success, ever since.

Legitimisation of the status quo
86 There are very few societies, if any, in the world that have not in some form sought legitimisation from the religious bodies within their midst. The partnership of priest and politician is not a phenomenon confined to Ancient Rome. This has not always been a cynical exploitation of religion by the State, nor self-seeking opportunism on the part of the religious communities. To confine our comments solely to Christianity, it is surely true that the great majority of Christians accept the fact that they are citizens of a particular country, with citizens' responsibilities. Many of them will take leadership responsibility at different levels within their society. Believing that all authority comes from God and is to be exercised in the spirit of Christ, they will take this responsibility seriously as a sacred trust.

87   Since politics, at any level, is 'the art of the possible' they will accept that they cannot always follow the Gospel precepts fully and will look upon the consequent compromises as inevitable. Yet they will always try to persuade people to see the validity of the principles. Further, they recognise that individuals need corporate checks, balances, sanctions, laws, structures and the like, both for support and for the limiting of human temptation to dominance. They may therefore accept such structures as currently exist in their society as being themselves God-given. From all these ingredients affirmation of the *status quo* is easily accepted and divine sanctions found for it. For instance the English religious tradition since the sixteenth century has laid great emphasis on prayer for the sovereign and for those that govern. With it has sometimes gone acceptance of 'the rich man in his castle and the poor man at his gate' as part of the God-given order of things. In this way religion is very often seen by ruling classes as supportive, cementing the fabric of society.

Christians and change

> Often in history a conservative church has opposed the new, eventually come to terms with it, found a Christian rationale for it and then become fiercely conservative about it.

88   To those holding such attitudes proposals for change can seem subversive and anti-Christ. Upheaval, violence and revolution will be opposed in the name of the God of peace and order. Those upholding the current order in society may forget that their forefathers opposed that order when it was innovative. Often in history a conservative Church has opposed the new, eventually come to terms with it, found a Christian or Gospel rationale for it, and then become fiercely conservative about it. There are also, of course, examples of where Christians have led the forces of change, for instance the seventeenth-century Puritans or contemporary base communities in Latin America. They have tried to replace one regime by a more godly one. Sometimes radical and conservative Christians are in conflict with each other. In public life today Christians will often be found on different sides of any debate.

89 However, despite the continuing involvement of many individual Christians in public life, and despite the perpetuation of the outward forms of the Church of England's 'established' status (Coronation, Assize Services, Prayers in Parliament and so forth), there has been a clear if subtle change in Church/State relations, not only in this country but across the Western world.

90 In examining that change it is helpful to follow Brian Horne in making a distinction between the three concepts of *State, Society* and *Culture.*

'The notions are all closely related but they are also different. Within a culture a society finds its place, and within a society a state takes shape. A culture is the complex pattern of shared apprehensions, beliefs and ideas which is passed on from generation to generation. A society is the more or less identifiable nexus of human relationships which is moulded by and expresses that tradition. A state is the concrete expression of the society for the purpose of its everyday, orderly organisation. It can be both an expression of the culture and also a perversion of the culture.' [10]

Dr Horne has also reminded us of Eliot's view that, within an overall Christian culture, a society can be itself Christian, non-Christian (Eliot uses the term 'pagan'), or neutral, i.e. 'mixed'. In the third case, however, it will always be in process of becoming *more* Christian or *more* pagan. There are of course occasions when the Church feels it necessary to distance itself to some extent from the state, and the latter sometimes resents this. But on the whole the Church seems to act in the belief that unless it uses every opportunity presented to it (including the privileges of establishment) to seek to maintain its inheritance of Christian culture then British society will move inexorably from its present 'mixed' position to one of outright 'paganism'.

Britain's multi-cultural heritage
91 An alternative view might be that there is no longer any such thing as a *single* British, or even English, culture – even if there ever has been. When Eliot described British society in the 1930s as straddling the whole spectrum from Christian through neutral to pagan, though tending towards the latter, was he perhaps describing the situation not merely in his own day but as it had in fact been for at least two hundred and fifty years (since the collapse of the Commonwealth) or even longer?[11] But however one may interpret the past there can surely be no doubt

that the current scene shows a very different relationship between Church and State from that monolithic inter-dependence which Henry VIII attempted to create.

92 The traditional inter-relation, however partial, of faith and culture has already largely disappeared in most European countries. As we have already seen (in Chapter 3) the cultural atmosphere created by such a process of secularisation tends to make religious belief and morality a *private* rather than a *social,* or *public,* matter and so it is more difficult for religious belief and moral values to be adopted by people at large. The position is further complicated, however, because cultures in modern complex societies have become fragmented and separated from one another, so that most of us tend to belong to a variety of sub-cultures within an overall culture. For example, the sub-culture of our work-place may well be very different from the sub-culture of our family, or of our leisure pursuits. One needs to ask what the implications of all this are for the claim which is often made that 'faith must become culture, if it is to be fully received and lived'.[12]

> 'Faith must become culture if it is to be fully received and lived'
>
> When cultural identity has a religious component the emergence of any apparent threat can cause emotions to boil over.

93 One of the arguments lying behind such a claim will presumably be that culture, like genuine faith, has to do with the roots of our identity. It is in this sense that *cultures,* as opposed to sub-cultures, still exert their major force on their individual members. Strong emotions are aroused when people feel their cultural identity is in danger of being destroyed. When that cultural identity also has a religious component the emergence of any apparent threat can cause emotions to boil over. The examples of Northern Ireland and the Middle East are but the most obvious examples of this at the present time.

The Church's own structures and activity within society

94 Even though the process of secularisation is well advanced in many westernised countries, the churches themselves have not always submitted to what might seem to be its necessary consequences. In Britain in particular, where Established Churches still exist, the parochial system is still fully entrenched. In many places, what is more, it is still effective in maintaining a traditional relationship between the church and the local community. Weddings and funerals, Town Council annual Services, and village fetes, for example, still act as expressions of that relationship.

95 The essential feature of the parochial system is that it places upon the clergy and congregation of the parish church a responsibility for *all* those living within the parish boundaries. It is, of course, a concept which in practice is not confined to the Church of England. Many congregations seek to ensure that when people in their local area are in trouble steps are taken to demonstrate practical caring – by going with them to the DSS, or to court, for example – and so expressing the love of Christ in action.

96 Sometimes, especially in UPA parishes, the churches provide the only place where people of varied ethnic origins can freely come together. For example, a large group of Barbadians worship at St Peter's within Coventry East Team ministry, and a group of Indian Christians are an important part of the congregation of St Paul's, Foleshill, Coventry. These churches also have important links with other community organisations and provide through their buildings some of the places where people can meet.

The Church and local government

> Parish churches have often provided local
> residents with a 'voice' to protest.

97 Involvement in the local community can lead to using the structures of local government. Parish churches have often provided local residents with a 'voice' to protest against what they find undesirable for their area. For instance, one UPA parish which joined in a local residents' group set up to lobby the City Council because it was failing to

meet a number of local needs found that it was the committed church members that had the tenacity to keep going throughout what proved to be a very lengthy process indeed. 'It was our faith that enabled us to stick.'

98 Similarly, St Barnabas, Red Lane, also part of Coventry East Team, was a small struggling church nearly condemned to closure like many other inner city churches in the early 1970s. However, it successfully led the opposition to an unnecessary by-pass road cutting through its parish, and then went on to adapt its buildings in order to provide appropriate care for families and old people. Now, with help from the Church Urban Fund, the buildings have been made into a resource for people of many creeds and none.

99 In these and similar ways the Church can still influence the culture and the society of which it is part. A more direct impact, however, can perhaps be made through the Church's long-established involvement in the educational system of the country. What the children are taught in school, and *how* they are taught, clearly has a major influence on the direction a culture takes. So too does the character of the public media. In so far as the Church is still able to influence the climate created by press and broadcasting, so it is able to help shape future cultural development.

Prophetic challenge
100 Even though the Church will seek to use the opportunities presented by its involvement in the structures of society there will still be occasions when it will need to take a critical stand on the very edge of those structures, and possibly even to move outside them altogether. Third World 'base communities' present a striking model of the church structured for alternative community action, and a few parishes in this country find themselves needing to develop similar experiments for their own immediate areas.

101 As well as acting outside the conventional structures of society, the Church feels impelled from time to time to 'speak out' about certain of its features. Examples of what might rather dramatically be called 'prophetic denunciation' of such features by those within the Church can be found in relation to issues of war, the uses of nuclear power, business morality, economic goals, and attitudes to trade with under-developed countries, whether by governments or multi-national companies.

Its impact through evangelism

> Concentrating efforts not on social, cultural
> or political activities, but on 'straight-
> forward evangelism'.

102   There are many within the churches who will argue that the only
real impact the Church can make on any society is through the personal
conversion of the individual members of that society. They will therefore concentrate their efforts not on social, cultural, or political activities,
but on 'straight-forward evangelism'. We will examine later in the
Report the range of meaning which is appropriate to that word 'evangelism'. But it is at least arguable that before concentrating its efforts a
parish will need to consider a whole range of related questions concerning the possible ways of opening up the local community to the
impact of the Gospel. Those who claim to be interested only in 'straight-
forward' evangelism may be out of touch with their neighbours. They
may try to overcome this difficulty by starting up clubs etc with the
specific purpose of providing links into the community. Their ultimate
goal of bringing people to Christ is not in dispute, but unfortunately
Christian friendliness and caring can often be seen as suspect by those
on the receiving end. 'Do they really care for me, or do they just want
to recruit me?'

103   Looking back in history the English Church has often tried to build
on what is there, to 'baptise' existing customs into a Christian meaning.
As Lord Runcie has said[13] *'Ours is a Church of the smoking flax .... of the
mixture of wheat and tares .... We leave it to the Lord to sort out the wheat
from the tares; for our part we are committed to fan the smoking flax into the
fire of faith. We are equipped for complexity because our tradition is to cast
evangelism in the mould of pastoral care .... In our history God has worked to
keep our borders open .... We seek to proclaim the Gospel with simplicity, but
simplicity is often the product of a stored and ordered mind.'* The next three
chapters of our Report seek to explore further the questions pointed up
by Dr Runcie's remarks, questions which have been implicit in the
mainly descriptive paragraphs above, but which now need more de-
tailed exploration.

Chapter 7

GOSPEL AND CULTURE: AFFIRMATION OR CONFRONTATION?

Is the Gospel 'for' or 'against' culture?
104 It has been noted above that societies have always tended to look to religion to 'legitimise' their activities. How should Christians respond to any such expectation on the part of the society of which they are members? Is it right to expect the Christian Gospel to fulfil the function of a 'religion' in this sense? And even if it is, can the Church commit itself to the affirming of any particular society or culture come what may? New Testament teaching on the relationship between the Kingdom, the Church and the World would suggest that Christians can offer no permanent, unqualified commitment to any human institution – not even to the Church itself. On the other hand, Christians cannot simply shrug off all responsibility for the well-being of the society in which they live. We are therefore faced with the question: 'How does the Church find the right balance between supporting or affirming culture and confronting it with the Gospel challenge?'

105 Canon Sam Van Culin in *Anglican Information*, No 56, Sept 89, writes:

> Each language and its related culture can be
> a means of opening individuals to the Word of
> God and to the gift of life in Christ. But at the
> same time the Word of God is an irruption into
> culture and human history. As such it challenges
> each man and woman in every culture by calling
> us to new values which may be at variance with
> our heritage. This point of paradox and tension
> is where Anglicans have often been in their
> history and where they belong.

106 Jesus lived as a first century Jew, speaking Aramaic in a land occupied by the Romans. The society of his day had an uneasy rapprochement between the Jewish religion, the puppet king Herod and the occupying authorities. He upheld the Jewish religion and culture, yet he also sought to reform it by insisting on the God-given principles which it was meant to enshrine. Similarly he obeyed the occupying power but with an absolute fidelity to God, whose prime authority put the lesser authorities in their place. This fidelity brought Jesus to the crucifixion. Thus began a process which eventually led to a new order, only ever partially enshrined in any particular culture, but exhibited by followers of Jesus in various modes and degrees.

The need to make choices
107 The Gospel is a way of life springing out of union with the God whom Jesus showed us. A way of life cannot be lived in a vacuum. Those following the way of Christ will sometimes see their discipleship requiring them to stand out against the culture around them, often challenging it, sometimes upholding it, or parts of it, often having to tolerate for a while things they cannot change immediately and sometimes experiencing a full coming together of the way of Christ and the culture around them. When to uphold or tolerate and when to challenge or oppose absolutely is always a difficult discernment. In some situations it has been a life and death discernment for his followers as it was for Jesus himself whether refusing to offer incense to the Emperor in the first three Christian centuries, or following the Christian way in certain totalitarian regimes today.

108 A startling example of an occasion when one Church leader felt it necessary to tolerate the prevailing culture while another felt it necessary to challenge it is given in Galatians 2.11-end. It had long been accepted that Jews and Gentiles could not eat together. The first Christians were unclear whether, because of the coming of Christ, this rule still applied. Peter was among those who had come to accept the new principle that believers of both origins *could* eat together, but he decided in certain particular circumstances to eat only with Jews. On hearing of this, Paul vehemently denounced him as jeopardising the very freedom of the Gospel. For him far too much was at stake to tolerate this pre-Christian custom even for a particular time with particular people.

> The segregation of men and women at
> social events, meetings or religious assemblies
> is common in many cultures.

109   In his paper to the 1988 Lambeth Conference[14] Bishop David Gitari raises a similar issue by describing a situation which he suggests 'though not consistent with the Gospel, could be tolerated for the time being'. The segregation of men and women in social situations, at meetings or in religious assemblies for instance, is common in many cultures. In a particular African tribe custom forbade men to be present at any assembly with women. Consequently the evangelist who came among them had initially to conduct a women's service and then to follow it by one for men. St Paul's words from Galatians 3.28 ('There is no such thing as Jew and Greek, slave and freeman, male and female; for you are all one person in Christ Jesus') could be seen to challenge the custom and require all to sit down together, but for the evangelist it was necessary to go along with the situation until a shift in the tribe's perception enabled a closer approximation to the Gospel ideal.

New challenges
110   Throughout Church history there have been similar periods of accommodation. There has to be a certain pragmatic opportunism in the strategy of the Church. A small minority Church can have little influence on cultural norms. The first Christians apparently raised no challenge to the institution of slavery (though Col 3.11 could be read as a fundamental undermining of the institution) but in nineteenth century Europe the slave trade was at last overthrown in the name of the Gospel. The Gospel does its work, even while the Church tolerates unChristian practices, by constantly confronting society with the ideal.

> 'If they are to remain here they must become
> like us'.
> But for a Muslim religion and culture cannot
> be separated

111   Many would see similar Gospel revolutions in the contemporary redefining of the place of women in society and in the establishment in

the western world of multi-ethnic and multi-faith societies. In Britain this is currently more apparent in inner city areas than in rural or suburban areas, but the situation is changing. As the gap widens between rich and poor, encouraged by the enterprise culture, increasing numbers of Asians move up the social ladder and out of the inner cities. It is changing too, because of the higher profile of Muslims, symbolised by the Salman Rushdie affair. This raises sharply the relationship between culture and religion. There are demands from many, including government ministers, for integration of all immigrant communities into 'British Culture'; 'if they are to remain here, they must become like us'. From the Muslim community there are increasing calls for a status within British society which recognises their religion as distinct, protects it from abuse, and allows its members to bring up their families according to particular norms. For a Muslim, religion and culture cannot be separated.

112   This brings us back yet again to the question of how far religion and culture can be separated within the Christian tradition. It is obviously not necessary to be British in order to be a Christian. Is it any more necessary to be a Christian in order to be British? Or, to put the question in a less naive form, to what extent is British culture today supportive of Christianity? Will further changes in Britain in a multicultural direction undermine the work of the Gospel?

The universality of the Gospel
113   In an international context, of course, the Gospel has for centuries flourished in a variety of cultures. In his Lambeth paper Bishop Gitari gives an attractive picture of the beauty of African music, drama and dance used to express the Gospel. He shows how this contributes to the fullness of Christ's body worldwide. This principle is not limited to artistic expression. The Bishop also speaks of the African perception of the individual as having unique personality, yet being so much part of the corporate as to come to the fullness of that personality only within the corporate. This he sees as being a valuable corrective to Westernised individualism.

114   Certain Christians have always rejoiced when they find human behaviour and insights, from whatever source, congruent with the Gospel. Customs which were originally pagan have been reinterpreted as Christian. Human attitudes in general have been taken as being expressive of Christian truths. Such an approach will be defended on the grounds that since every human perception of truth is partial, every

Christian perception must itself be partial. Moreover, the Christian vision of the new humanity in Christ, with every human perspective redeemed and contributing, remains a goal achievable only through welcoming and receiving diversity. Thus the dialogue within and between cultures can, indeed must, contribute to the wholeness in Christ.

Being called *out of* the world

115 There is another strand which has manifested itself in the Christian tradition. From New Testament times a contrast has sometimes been drawn between God's kingdom and 'the world'. The world is seen as 'society organised apart from God', that is godless, evil and ruled by the devil. There have always been some Christians who have equated 'the world' in this sense with the particular society and culture surrounding them. They have therefore seen their evangelistic task as being to call people *out* of the world into the fellowship of believers. They see human nature as fatally flawed, if not totally corrupt, and individuals and society equally flawed, corrupt and subject to death and destruction. They maintain a permanent contrast between human nature and divine grace, human reason and divine revelation, human society and the company of the saved.

> 'It is not the world which will be redeemed, but believing individuals who are called out of it.'

116 One corollary of this is a belief that the special, infallible revelation given to Christians includes a way of life which they are to follow strictly, refusing all compromise with society around them. Christians therefore have no need to be concerned with politics or the affairs of this world for it is not the world which will be redeemed, but believing individuals who are called out of it. It is accepted, however, that though Christians are not of the world, they do have for the time being to live in it. A preference may actually be expressed for one kind of society rather than another, usually the settled society which does not interfere with their practice of religion. It may even be accepted that Christians are permitted to make a good living out of the world by their diligent application, even though they must still see all material things as transitory. Their call is to live the Gospel life despite the temptations of the world.

117 Extreme sects illustrate this attitude most clearly, but it is not entirely confined to them. It is a strand which runs through many perceptions which claim Christian roots, although with varying degrees of distortion or misapplication of Gospel insights.

Testing the alternatives

118 The positions of accepting culture (114) and rejecting it (115f) are at opposite poles. There are a variety of positions in between. The Gospel renews what is good in culture and transforms what needs to be changed. As in all life, continual dying and rising, leaving behind and reaching forward, is the pattern of growth. We believe the attitude of Christians to the cultures which surround them must take fully into account the 'Signs of Authenticity' suggested in Chapter 5. If any aspect of a surrounding culture reflects any one of those 'signs' then the imperatives of the Gospel require the Church at least to 'maintain dialogue' with that area of thought or activity. Where the 'signs' are substantially present, then it will be right to seek to use it positively as a vehicle of the Gospel – or indeed welcome it as its own evidence of God's word at work in the world. Where such 'signs' are scarce, or missing altogether, then the imperatives of the Gospel will call for that aspect of the culture (or the society embodying that culture) to be challenged.

Chapter 8

WITNESSING TO THE GOSPEL IN OUR SOCIETY

Three approaches

119 It was suggested at the end of the previous chapter that the imperatives of the Gospel will lead the Church, according to circumstances, *either* to co-operate with the structures of a particular culture, *or* to oppose them directly. They will of course *also* lead the Church at all times to engage in evangelistic dialogue with individuals within that culture, and indeed with the culture itself. The following three sections explore those three approaches.

120 Discerning which approach is appropriate in any given situation will not always be easy. Our discernment will depend on how we evaluate the culture and how we experience the Gospel. Different people will advocate one approach rather than another with varying degrees of enthusiasm, but the essential point to bear in mind is that in most circumstances it is perfectly reasonable, and indeed necessary, for the Church to engage in all three approaches at one and the same time.

Social concern within the structures of society

> ... day care centres, job creation schemes, race relations, out of school children's groups, police liaison, clubs for young offenders on probation, etc.

121 It is heartening to encounter a number of imaginative ways in which churches, especially those in UPAs, have become involved with the life of the local area: day care centres, job creation schemes, race relations, out of school children's groups, police liaison, clubs for young offenders on probation, etc. Such initiatives spring from, and are authentic signs of, the gospel, offering human resources for the overcoming of deprivation and lack of power, displaying acceptance of people as

they are and seeking to bring reconciliation between different people and groups. There are many other examples of this type of Christian care, which is seen as a way of sharing the love of Christ, and enabling people to *hear* the good news that Christ cares for them.

122 As well as inner city parishes there are examples in UPA housing estates where the involvement of clergy and lay people in the community over the years has established a kind of credibility for the church. It has become 'good news' in the community. In St John's, Willenhall, Coventry, the sharing of leadership in worship is symbolic of the sharing of leadership as a whole within the church and the wider community. In this parish the follow-up to *Faith in the City* continues a tradition of involvement in community organisations, such as the Police Liaison Committee and the Community Centre. The city, the bishop, the diocese and cathedral and other organisations (among them Barclays Bank) have provided funds for a variety of projects. One of these is designed to promote the economic regeneration of the area; another enables city council officials to consult the local people when decisions are being made. When people begin to feel that their advice is important, they experience this as a form of liberation, and for them that is good news.

123 The crucial issue about these projects is whether they are a reversion to unhelpful patterns of doing things for other people. If so they simply trap everyone involved in a cycle of dependency which is not consonant with the Gospel. If on the other hand they are designed to enable people to help themselves and to deal more effectively with their own needs, they liberate people from their own past, both those who are the so-called experts or consultants and those who might appear to be merely recipients.

Challenging its norms and assumptions

124 As Paul's letters remind us (e.g. Rom 13) Christians have always seen a positive need to support authority and order; the rule of law holds human evil in check. But Christians have equally from time to time felt it in conscience necessary to challenge, oppose and even subvert regimes. Sometimes this will take the extreme form, where a regime is essentially evil in its nature, of working to overthrow it. More often, however, the Church's opposition will be take the form of challenging certain assumptions upon which a government conducts its programme. It is not only assumptions on the part of a government which

the Church may feel the need to challenge. Quite often the assumptions of a whole national culture appear to be inconsistent with the message of the Gospel. Two contemporary issues we take as examples:

(a) Challenging contemporary sexual morality and attitudes to marriage; and

(b) Challenging some aspects of the Enterprise Culture.

In neither issue is the matter simple.

Challenging certain patterns of behaviour

125 Some preachers will often talk about 'the breakdown of personal morality and of family life', (perhaps giving some statistics). And he (or she) may likewise cite the materialistic, consumerist, selfish attitude to life which is all around us. Presumably the purpose is to lead people to acknowledge guilt before pointing them to penitence and faith in the Saviour. But the same person outside the pulpit, and especially in a pastoral context, may find it less appropriate to challenge individuals directly either about their sexual morality or about their attitude to material things. Part of the reason is that the pastor will be looking for the least detrimental option for people in their personal plight; part is that he or she knows people don't accept the Church's norms and are frightened of them; and part because in both the instances cited the reality is complex.

126 Take first the attitude to family life in present day British society. Although one in three marriages are likely to end in divorce this is hardly grounds for predicting the imminent collapse of the institution of matrimony. Moreover, consideration of the figures concerning marriage and family life in a recent European survey suggests that most people still subscribe to a moral code close to the last seven commandments. The vast majority, nine out of ten, of men and women expect to marry at some point in their lives and to have children. Nevertheless, as we noted in para.33, the divorce rate in England and Wales has risen six-fold in the last twenty years.

127 These and the other statistics quoted in Chapter 3 may be interpreted in various ways. They are in no way a prescription for complacency, but neither do they seem a cause for despair. They provide an example of human imperfection, rather than a manifesto of revolt against Christian ideals of marriage. What sort of response is called for from the Church? Is it enough to point out that the present

situation shows the age-old gap between any statement of values and their performance, and that this has traditionally been identified within the Christian fellowship as sin, for which the traditional remedy is repentance, forgiveness and amendment of life, available to all as the fruits of the death and resurrection of Christ? Is it more appropriate under present circumstances simply to offer counselling and care to those hurt by current practice, and to set aside any talk of sin? Or should the Church denounce the present culture, and seek by whatever means is in its power, including parliamentary and legal measures, to stem the present trends? Or perhaps there is a different way to 'challenge' the present culture. What has developed in the wake of two world wars is the lack of any consensus about *why* ethical values in the fields of individual and family life are important. The churches are now being asked by many people to give a lead to the community as to how a new consensus should be created within our nation. Here perhaps is a challenge to the Church's own traditional role in pastoral teaching and apologetics.

Challenging certain ideologies

128 A similar task of offering sympathetic and stimulating challenge to current thinking is facing the Church in the fields of social, economic and political affairs. Since 1979 much has been made of the revival of Britain as a nation once more motivated by the spirit of enterprise. Behind the revival has been the clearly spelt-out ideology propounded by the New Right philosophers such as Hayek and Nozick, and expounded politically by people like Sir Keith Joseph.

129 That attention is given in this report to the capitalism of the New Right is not because of any assumption on our part that it is inevitably inimical to Christian principles (though this *is* a view held by some). It is simply that it happens to be the system which held the political high ground for some years. Such scrutiny would need to be given to whatever politico-economic theory was the dominant force in a culture under examination, whether it were Marxism, socialism or a different form of capitalism.

130 Three issues which the New Right philosophers have addressed are freedom, social justice and community. Fundamental to New Right thinking is the concept of the free market where goods and services are provided to match consumer demand. Competition will necessarily lead to efficiency and innovation. In order for the market mechanisms

to work effectively, people must be free to determine how to dispose of their own incomes. If they are taxed heavily by the State, their choices are restricted, and the incentive to work hard is undermined.

> 'Markets are much more like the weather
> in that outcomes are not foreseen or intended.'

131 The practice of compulsory distribution of income between people cannot be countenanced by New Right thinking. If some people grow poorer as a result of the 'impersonal' mechanisms of the market, they cannot be said to suffer an injustice. Whether the cause is their own incapacity for productive work or a fall in the market which reduces the rewards for their goods or services, there is no injustice. 'Although they embody human actions, markets are much more like the weather in that outcomes are not foreseen or intended'. In New Right philosophy the role of the State is limited to the maintenance of internal law and order and external defence in order to ensure that the pursuit of certain ends by one individual does not violate the rights of other individuals pursuing their own different ends. The primary purpose of the State must be to set its citizens free to pursue their own good. The government of a free society must be neutral over what constitutes a good life, and must not impose values. Even less must it compel its citizens to give up part of what is properly theirs for it to be redistributed to other people. In the most uncompromising versions of the philosophy, taxation to support welfare provision is thereby excluded. People who have been unfortunate or who have suffered from the unintended consequences of the market have no right of appeal to the wider society for support. They must instead seek to excite the freely chosen altruism of others in the form of charitable giving. Few, of course, would press the argument to such conclusions.

The need for debate
132 New Right philosophy has had profound influences on Government policy in the last decade, but it would be wrong to suppose that it has been translated into action in its entirety. Britain does not have a free market in the strict sense. If that were the case, restrictions on pollution, and health and safety measures would have been considerably reviewed. The State in Britain still continues to fund the major part of welfare provision out of general taxation, although it has moved

away from being the primary provider of services and has actively encouraged other forms of welfare provision through, for example, the voluntary sector.

133 Christians have found themselves divided in their attitudes to the New Right philosophies, but agree that there needs to be continuing debate about the ideas of freedom, social justice and community. A biblical understanding of freedom, for example, is that human beings are most free when they are at one with God in his purposes, unhampered by enslavement to 'the elemental powers', which have been conquered by Christ. Economic and market forces do not have unchallenged, unrestricted sovereignty; only under God's rule can they truly serve human interests. New Right thinking on social justice and community appears to be at odds with New Testament belief in fellowship (*koinonia*). Support for enterprise, initiative and hard work, can be derived from the New Testament but there they are always set within the context of the common good, the common welfare.

134 The debate needs to go on. For it is clear that wealth creation is essential if everyone is to benefit and if the essential functions of the State are to be maintained. It is clearly not the case, however, that the fruits of prosperity 'trickle down' automatically to the most deprived section of the population. If benefits, concessions and services to this group are at the same time reduced – especially if rewards and tax concessions to the achievers are simultaneously raised – the rich become richer and the poor poorer. This is evidenced by present statistics.[15]

Politics, economics and theology
135 Other systems of wealth creation, however, are conspicuously failing to produce adequate goods and services. In any case people should be expected to exercise individual responsibility as stewards of the material universe and co-creators with God; initiative needs encouraging. In the operation of any system the consequences of human failings and 'original sin' are obvious; the system needs both to recognise this and to limit its damaging effect. Again, in any system the absence of shared values and morals or of any unifying vision of society heightens the political dilemma facing that society.

136 A theology which works at situations realistically, asking where God is at work in them, brings energy and moral value to human efforts at co-operation. We look for a time when the application of theology to

political thinking will not only bring forward criticisms of existing systems but will seek to pioneer alternative systems and ideologies. Theology may never discover a political ideal which everyone can accept, but it needs to be in the forefront of the search for such. Those who find the present political ideology and economic practice unsatisfactory might join those who are engaged in seeking for alternatives, for this too is part of the Church's task of evangelisation of the culture within which we live.

> Any system which encourages attitudes out of keeping with, or foreign to, the Gospel needs confronting not legitimising

137   Some leaders in the new enterprise culture may criticise the Churches for failing to legitimise the current ideology. But many in the Churches believe that naked individualistic competitiveness is a moral evil which undermines values of stability, fidelity and other family and community-building values, and that the frenetic pace of life militates against human reflectiveness and wholeness. A system which encourages such attitudes needs confronting, not legitimising. Inter-action and inter-dependence come from God's very nature as Three-in-One and are reflected in all that is, most especially in human nature. God has united himself with human nature to show the possibility of a new humanity. Accepting the consequences of human alienation and antagonism, he demonstrates love as superior to all negativity and shares power for a new quality of life. The doctrines of God, Creator, incarnate, crucified-risen, giving Holy Spirit to build the new humanity are the core of Christian faith. Discovery of how this faith intersects with all of life's circumstances is the ground of Christian hope. Christians will not be over-confident that they have the answers, but they may certainly have confidence in the God who enables people to work out at least the next step in the process.

When and how to tell the Good News
138   The verb 'to evangelise' in New Testament usage means literally 'to proclaim the good news'. Neither of the nouns 'evangelism' or 'evangelisation' appears as such. In Roman Catholic circles the noun 'evangelisation' is frequently used in a comprehensive sense that includes both the social work and the prophetic challenge described in

this chapter. Most of this report can be said to relate to evangelisation in this wider sense The noun 'evangelism' is often used with a more focused meaning. As we say in Chapter 5, the focus of the Gospel is the story of the life, death, resurrection and ascension of Jesus Christ, and so evangelism must include the encouragement of individuals and groups to link their story to that story, in the hope that all may experience personal and social transformation in becoming committed disciples.

139 We have already seen how such a process raises a number of cultural questions. Chapter 3 examined the entry points for the Gospel in different cultures and stressed the alien feel to much church culture. Chapter 4 described the task of identifying the form of the Good News appropriate for each context and Chapter 9 will examine how far there must be a break from previous cultural and religious experience when an individual or a group takes on a discipleship commitment.

140 It must be admitted that the word 'evangelism' itself arouses conflicting responses, even among Christians. For some it simply identifies the primary task of the church, the proclamation of the good news of Christ to people who have not heard of him, or have a very confused idea of his significance. For others it is a word associated with activities which they consider arouse opposition and rejection rather than interest and commitment. That does not mean that they are not concerned to share their faith with those around them *in an appropriate way*, but they see the problem of working out what *is* an appropriate way as a *real* problem in today's society.

Evangelism through meeting needs
141 One Anglican PCC, after a Ministry Development Programme, set itself to discuss what evangelism was and what a local church should do about it. Eventually they decided that evangelism was a responsibility of each and every one of their committees whether communications, education, social, buildings or whatever. One of the churchwardens summed it up: 'We used to think that evangelism was telling people that we had a lively programme of worship and social life in our church and asking them to join us. Now we know that it means that we have to go and find people where they are in need and try to serve them for Jesus' sake, and if they start to come to church (as many of them do) that is an added bonus'. That particular church, like many others, started a coffee morning for mothers with young toddlers, because they had worked out that these were the people most in need in that

particular parish. Occasionally the opportunity arose for a gentle and sensitive sharing of faith. As a result of that care and concern a number of these young families started attending church on a Sunday. But that was not the *motive* for the concern; it was not a subterfuge to encourage church growth.

142 That interpretation of evangelism takes seriously the suggestion that any overt proclamation of the Gospel needs to be in the context of wider 'evangelisation'. Where there is a ministry to the needs of a group in the community without explicitly naming the name of Christ, some would prefer, for the sake of clarity, to use the term 'mission' rather than 'evangelism'. 'Evangelism' as such must surely normally involve the use of words (see *The Measure of Mission*, page 38).

143 While there is a danger of insensitive evangelism that proclaims a pre-packaged message and is impatient with the call for friendship and dialogue, there is also the danger of retreating into a ghetto with the excuse that 'it is all so difficult'. It is as we reach out in friendship that we can learn the sensitivity of approach that is needed. Faithfulness to the whole calling of Christ impels us to share the message of Jesus Christ through whom alone the vicious circles of enmity, guilt, fear and hopelessness are broken. It is certain that when this message is truly heard, believed and acted upon, it brings the hope of breaking through that sense of bondage and oppression which afflicts so many in our society today, that sense of despair among those who feel they have been abandoned or have somehow failed in their lives.

Bridge or barrier?
144 One of the central questions in the practice of evangelism and in our report as a whole is to ask how far the Gospel accepts people as they are (as well as *where* they are) and how far it confronts them with the need for immediate transformation. It is a central theological question, but it is also an acute pastoral problem. The Gospel calls us to love our neighbour as ourselves; love involves friendship and understanding, and accepting people where they are, not imposing our values upon them. It involves standing by them when they are down, using our inherited resources to provide for their rights. How does one present the Good News of a loving and accepting God while being equally true to the Gospel's challenge to repentance and change of lifestyle? This is particularly difficult when relating to popular or 'folk' religion. The fact that a large percentage of the population of this

country believes in God and prays can be welcomed as providing a bridge to the Gospel, but some argue that this rudimentary belief can in practice be a barrier to more explicit faith in Christ.

145 Before commenting directly on that argument we need to return to the important, though less central, issue of church growth. Some forms of evangelism give the impression that the goal is simply to recruit new members to our particular sector of the Church. Others have reacted to this danger by placing such an emphasis on God's presence and activity in the world that there seems to be little place in their theology of evangelism for the Christian community. An attempt to strike a balance between the two extremes is to speak of the Gospel as being about new life in a new community that is open to the world and is both transformed and transforming. Membership of the community is *part* of the goal of evangelism, but problems arise when, as is often the case, the local expression of that community is neither transformed nor transforming, being closed to the world by virtue of its own unfamiliar sub-culture.

> Evangelism is not simply, or even primarily, about recruiting new members to the Christian community.

146 However, evangelism is not simply or even primarily about recruiting new members to the Christian community; it is nothing less than the transformation of persons and situations. In seeking such transformation some churches are more positive towards 'folk' religion than others. It can clearly be an effective bridge to the Gospel, but there are accompanying aspects of popular religion that are less positive – such as the danger of self-sufficiency and the desire to manipulate God for one's own ends. It has to be acknowledged of course, that these aspects are present within the church as well as outside. Many suburban churches, for example, could be said to have more affinity with the principles of a capitalist society than with the New Testament. This has been described as mixing a privatised gospel of personal forgiveness with a worldly attitude to wealth and power.

The importance of context
147 When we look at the example of Jesus himself in this matter we see that he was primarily accepting of those who had been rejected by

society, those who were poor in the material sense or those like Zacchaeus who were aware of their spiritual poverty. He brought confrontation, however, to many of the powerful religious leaders. The balance of acceptance and confrontation seems to have varied according to context, and according to the stage reached in a person's discipleship. He initially allowed the crowds to be attracted by his ministry of acceptance, healing and grace, but he later confronted them with a challenge that caused many to withdraw (John 6 – esp. v.66).

148   The context is therefore key to finding the right balance of acceptance and confrontation. In the wrong circumstances a presentation of the Gospel that focuses primarily on challenge may become alienating rather than attractive and imply an emphasis on works rather than on grace. The right initial approach is one of contextualisation, enabling people to respond meaningfully to the Gospel from within the framework of their own situation. But when contextualisation stresses the accepting element of the Gospel to the exclusion of its confrontational element it becomes syncretism.

149   So far we have been discussing the issue in relation to the question of 'folk religion', but it is of course wider than that. When the gospel calls us to evangelism, to preach the good news of the saving power of Jesus Christ, this is for the whole of humanity, not just for those who happen to be born into Western culture. This demand used to be satisfied by sending people and money to 'the mission field'. It is increasingly recognised that mission frontiers are to be found everywhere and that parts of Africa, for example, are now more Christian than most of Britain.

> The good news of the saving power of Jesus Christ is for the whole of humanity

150   Particular questions arise when there are adherents of other faiths in our local community. It is often the churches in inner city areas, which are weakest in numbers and finance – but not, it must clearly be said, in commitment – who are faced with the questions most squarely. But we are one church, following the one Lord, given the same mission imperative. Therefore these are questions which face us all, whether we have members of other faiths as immediate neighbours or not. How

can we fulfil this imperative of our Lord without trampling on people's cultures, and on the good things that are obviously there, for those who care to look, in their cultures and indeed in their religions?

The way of dialogue
151 In seeking a solution to this problem many people find that the word 'dialogue' offers a way forward. The word implies a real meeting between people, as individuals *and as communities*. It means a listening to each other, and a mutual witness to religious faith amongst other things. There is of course a danger that it can mean anything and everything. We need to ask a number of questions about how people are using the term. Is it *a* means of evangelism? Or is it *the* means of evangelism? Is it mission, but not evangelism? Ultimately, however, it is a term of real value. As *The Measure of Mission* says (page 41), true dialogue means trusting others enough to share one's most valued beliefs with them. In this sense it is both witness and evangelism.

152 These theological questions face all of us. Direct experience with people who have converted to Christianity from another major faith has raised particular questions concerning the relationship between their old religious and cultural world and the new one which they have entered. In terms of a person's previous cultural identity, what is required of such people as they take on new commitments and loyalties? These are centred on Jesus Christ and baptism into his Name, but he or she is also becoming a member of the body of Christ, i.e. entering a church which will have a very different cultural flavour from his or her previous world. What can remain continuous with that world, and where must breaks be made? By what criteria do we judge the relationship between a person's commitment to Jesus Christ and his or her culture in each case? This is complicated by the extreme difficulty in distinguishing religion and culture in all the major faiths (cf paras 15f). It is also a question to be addressed to ourselves, the receiving community. How, if at all, should we be willing to make adjustments, and real changes in our church life, worship and leadership, to accommodate converts from other faiths?

153 Some Christians would reject any suggestion that converts can bring into their new discipleship anything of value from their way of life before they met Christ. Such a view might seem to be fortified by the fact that quite often when someone is changed by an encounter with Jesus Christ, that person seems to want almost immediately to move

away from his or her background. This report has suggested that evangelism in the name of Jesus, if it is to be effective, needs to meet all people where they are, in their own culture. However, once they have been encountered there, the next question must inevitably arise; what can be affirmed in that culture, and what in the end has to be seen as incompatible with the Gospel?

Chapter 9

CONVERSION AND CONTINUITY

The importance of one's roots?

154 One way of framing the question posed at the end of the last chapter is to ask how far an evangelist can build on the experience of faith a person already has. The New Testament does not give a single clear answer to that question. In the Fourth Gospel we read that when Jesus approached the Samaritan woman he seemed to use what she had learnt from her own religious background (John, ch 4). A similar approach, according to Acts, was made by St Paul to the Greeks on the Areopagus (Acts 17). Yet there are many passages which seem to insist that there must be a complete break and a beginning again, a total movement from darkness to light, a being born again (John 3, 1 John etc). How far can the Church give a definitive, universally applicable answer to this question from a purely doctrinal basis? Or how far is it for each convert to answer for himself? There may be some things which have been real in his past experience, which he does not want to deny. There may be others which he wishes to put away, even if the Church says they are acceptable.

155 Then there is the further question as to how far evangelism should address whole families and communities. In pioneering Industrial Mission Bishop Ted Wickham never failed to emphasise the strategy of working with the group rather than the individual. The same approach is needed with Asian ethnic groupings. Should evangelism deliberately encourage individual commitment, often taking an individual out of his family and community altogether? Is the model to be the man born blind in John 9, who had to come out of his family, or the jailor in Acts 16, who was baptised with all his household? If it is to be the former, what are we doing to enable the Church to be the new family for the isolated convert? There is no one answer to these questions.

156 Converts from different religions will give various answers as to where they can affirm that there have been real experiences in their old faith which can be 'brought with them'. But the answers may also differ between converts from the same religion – on whether they feel, for

example, that the Sikh experience of God, and the place of the Guru in their tradition, can be seen as a preparation for Christian faith, or whether it must be completely put aside as misleading. They would also differ about whether the symbols of the Sikh faith must be totally set aside, or whether a convert can attend (and if so, in what way) the ceremonies associated with the marriage or death of any of his family remaining within the Sikh community. Similar questions could also be asked when dealing with the myriad of new religious movements, which have been attracting many of the young in recent years.

> Can a convert from the Sikh faith attend any
> of the ceremonies associated with the marriage
> or death of any of his family remaining
> within the Sikh community?

157   The Church's traditional approach would probably be to emphasise the need for a complete break, as a totally new life is taken in Christ. Those advocating this emphasis tend to see any other approach as a failure to follow the Great Commission (Mt 28.16-20) and offer the full Christian challenge to those from other faiths. In the alternative approach, which uses dialogue, there would be an attempt to explore *together* what is theologically acceptable and so can be continuous with the culture of the previous faith, and what must be discontinuous. The criterion would be the gospel of Jesus Christ, and what is meant by his being *the* Way, *the* Truth and *the* Life. Our evangelistic message must surely always be that it is *Christ* that we are offering – not a superior religion, but a person in whom the truth of God is most clearly shown through his life, death and resurrection, and in the New Testament witness to him.

Continuity preserved
158   As an example of a situation where dialogue *did* occur, let us look at the case of a particular Sikh convert who wishes to stress, not discontinuity, but continuity in his religious and cultural experience. He sees his upbringing as the foundation for what followed. He is still able to quote the Mantra which was his childhood statement of faith:

'There is one God. Eternal truth is his name. Creator of all things, and the all pervading Spirit. He is without fear. He is without enmity. He is timeless and formless – beyond births and deaths. He is self-enlightened. By the Grace of the Guru, He is made known.'

He is able to make direct links between this, and his being met by Jesus Christ, who has become in a real sense his Guru, showing him above all the picture of God who shares our humiliation and weakness. He links his earlier experience of serving God to the full in the Gurdwara with a new call to service to humanity through the Church.

159   This choice still brings all sorts of conflict in his family; but it is unavoidable as he feels the direct impact of the words of John 15.16 - 'You did not choose me. I chose you and appointed you to go and bear much fruit ... fruit that endures'. He has felt that part of that call has been to remain in touch with his community, through which his respect for them and their faith has grown rather than declined. He struggles to sit where they sit, and share at every level, theological, religious, and practical. He understands the position of his family, that they can worship God in the Gurdwara, as he is able to in the Church. His early life has shown him that it is the same God. He wears a steel bracelet – the Kara, one of the five Ks of the Sikh faith – as a sign of pride in his roots, and his respect for them. 'It is a sign of my commitment to stand for God's truth and the justice that demands. My Christian loyalty inspires my respect for my Sikh roots, rather than leading me to reject them.' His path in the church has not always been an easy one, nor unfortunately has there always been an Asian Christian fellowship in the locality to sustain him.

160   There are some who affirm the idea of 'continuity' so strongly that they argue against direct evangelism among those belonging to other faiths. They claim that there are different ways to God, and the lives of those who are strong in other faiths clearly show they know God at least as adequately as most Christians. The most extreme form of this view asserts that conversion is not to be welcomed even if it is asked for; that it is actually to be discouraged, as breaking up delicate balances in community relations and encouraging competition between religions. The Christian task, they argue, is to develop mutual understanding with those of other faiths so that we can live in harmony as religious people, and as fellow citizens of God's world. Others, while not going so far as actively to *discourage* conversion from another faith, believe that pragmatically we should not undertake any direct evangelism among those already committed to another faith because we need, particularly in our own society, to concentrate on those millions of people without any faith at all.

The central question

161 This debate poses, in perhaps its starkest form, the issue which underlies all the other questions which this report has been seeking to explore. *To what extent does the Gospel, the Word of God, manifest itself as universally active in the world, calling us to share work which is already in process, which needs to be discovered and recognised as well as forwarded? Or to what extent does God's Word actually depend upon the activity of the Church for its effective reception by the world?*

162 The more weight we give to the second of these positions, the greater stress will we place on preserving a separate 'Church culture', on calling for a clear rejection of all that belongs to non-Christian faiths and non-Christian cultures. We will seek constantly to 'confront' secular society, to pursue the 'conversion' of all who are not already within the Church (and perhaps even of some who are!) and will see conversion in terms of 'discontinuity' and change rather than of 'continuity' and growth. On the other hand the more weight we give to the concept of the Gospel being already active in the world, the more will our thinking be governed by the parable of the leaven rather than by the symbol of Noah's Ark. We will accept the possibility that the forms of the Gospel as we have inherited them may themselves be influenced by the cultural settings in which they developed, and so we will struggle to find appropriate forms which effectively convey the Good News of Jesus Christ to people in today's very different (and very varying) cultures.

163 The main thrust of this report has been in support of this second view, but it would be to misunderstand the situation completely to see the questions posed in paragraph 161 as being representative of alternative, opposing positions. Both questions start with the phrase 'To what extent...?' We would reject any approach which believed the answer to either question to be 'Completely'. In the midst of the unavoidable questions about cultural forms and the crucial need for bridge-building, we would uphold the need to keep in balance *both* aspects of the assertion that Christ who is 'the light that enlightens everyone' (John 1.9) also confronts people with the costly choice of whether or not they will be his disciples (Matthew 16 v.24).

PART C

Gospel, Culture and Church Life

Chapter 10

BAPTISMAL POLICIES

Earthing the issues

164   In para. 144 above we noted that the central question of that part of the Report was how far the Gospel accepts people as they are and how far it confronts them with the need for transformation. The current debate about baptismal policies illustrates a number of complex theological and pastoral issues arising out of that question.

165   Some parishes operate what is called an 'open' policy on infant baptism, others a 'restricted' policy. In the first instance the children of all residents are baptised, should they request it, whether or not the parents and family worship regularly at the parish church. The minister however, may request that the parents, and possibly the godparents, undergo a period of instruction on the nature and purpose of baptism into Christ as being made partakers of his death and resurrection, being made a child of God by adoption and being incorporated into his body, the Church.

166   In a parish with a 'restricted' policy baptism will be refused to children whose parents are not regular church attenders, unless and until they become worshippers for a period. They may, however, be offered a service of thanksgiving for the birth of the child, for which a service is provided in the 1980 *Alternative Service Book*, it being made plain to all participants that the Thanksgiving Service is not the equivalent of baptism.

Differing understandings

167   Both those who operate an 'open' policy and those who wish to be more 'restricted' argue their case in terms of a mission theology, but the two views express differing understandings of the relationship between culture and the Gospel. For some it is essential to the mission of the Church that the edges of the Church are blurred. That is what makes it easier for people to pass from non-commitment to commitment. For others it is necessary to make a clear distinction between those who have a strong commitment to the life and mission of the

Church and those who only occasionally attend its rites. This way, they believe, people will be challenged to turn away from a private interpretation of religion and take on the full responsibilities of discipleship.

168 When confronted with a 'restricted' policy parents often argue that it is possible to make a distinction between church attendance and belief in God, or indeed in the Trinity. 'Suffer little children....' is quoted, and feelings of rejection are expressed. The effect of refusal is not usually for the family to change its mind about churchgoing, but to request the bishop to allow another minister to baptise the child. Under such circumstance the bishop is bound to draw the incumbent's attention to Canon B 22 of the Church of England, to which every incumbent will have subscribed. Canon B 22 lays down the guidelines for baptismal policy for every parish and states that a minister may not refuse to baptise or unduly delay the baptism of an infant who is his parishioner. Preparation is encouraged, but refusal to baptise where preparation is resisted is not permitted.

169 The fact that preparation is encouraged is an implicit recognition that secularisation is bringing a transition in our culture at this time. The culture from which we are emerging held at its heart the model of 'Christendom' under which the whole community was expected to be baptised into the Church, whether they attend its functions or not. In contrast a secularised culture sees the Church as marginal to life, and baptism as therefore an act of significance only to those who have retained an interest in such matters. At present there is a steady decline in the practice of infant baptism. The *Alternative Service Book* seems to take the norm of Christian initiation to be the baptism and confirmation of adult believers, requiring promises which imply a deep and thoughtful commitment, though provision for Infant Baptism is of course made.

Differing theologies
170 As well as being aware of differing theologies of mission within the Church we have to acknowledge conflicting theologies of baptism itself. Some emphasise that baptism is a sign of God's utter patience and loving desire that all should experience salvation. Others emphasise the baptismal sign of dying to a life without God and rising to a new life in which Jesus is explicitly acknowledged as the Lord of the whole of life. Yet others would argue that baptism is the public acknowledgement that we are already children of God. These different views will issue in differing practices.

171   The fact that all recent ecumenical discussions of baptism indicate that explicit faith must accompany the act of initiation into Christ is used by some to argue for a more restricted position. They also stress that the Baptismal Promises, rightly understood, will involve a full commitment to serve Christ in the world. Others, arguing for a more open policy, while not denying the importance of commitment, believe it may grow slowly from an implicit stage. Certainly in the experience of the apostles and of many modern disciples the implications of an initial call are revealed only gradually. The defenders of an open policy also argue that God is constantly at work in the world, even where faith may be minimal. Moreover, they point out that, though some people have difficulty in articulating their faith, this does not mean they have none.

172   Although present diversities in practice can lead to conflict and confusion, in a stage of cultural transition this should not be a cause for surprise. Moreover it must always be remembered that we do not all live in the same culture today. In rural areas, where the Church is still often seen as integral to the local culture, infant baptism is still reasonably frequent. In inner city areas, however, where the Church is seen as unrelated or even alien to the local culture, infant baptisms are much rarer.

A broad path of agreement?

173   Given the diverse cultures, as well as differing theologies both of mission and of baptism, a single agreed policy by the Church would not seem possible at this time. However, if mission is the primary task of the Church, and we see the Gospel as both affirming and being critical of culture, then a general direction for future practice must emerge. The following considerations seem relevant to such a development.

174   Growing secularisation means that the Church has to pursue all the different missionary strategies required by the fact that fewer infants are being presented (or accepted) for baptism. For one thing, more people will offer themselves for baptism and confirmation together, thus opening up considerable opportunities for Christian teaching. On the other hand such requests for infant baptism as continue to be made should be taken seriously. The sincerity of the motivation of the family concerned should not be called into question. Some ministers will interpret this as a sign that faith already exists and through the contact and preparation will try to help the parents and god-parents to a fuller grasp of the meaning of the Gospel. They will see their willingness to baptise the child as a sign of God's acceptance of all who come to

him. Others, in cases where previous contact with the Christian faith seems to be almost non-existent, may delay making a decision whilst trying to build the parents into the life and witness of the Christian community. Where there is no positive response at all to the invitation to a greater identification with the Church, they may decide not to perform the sacrament, on the grounds that it could not possibly be a meaningful act for those taking part.

175   There can be no doubt that a glib acceptance of all without proper preparation is to treat the sacrament as a means of 'cheap grace'. It would look like capitulation to the modern pressure for easy credit where people are encouraged to get what they want instantly without being committed to anything beyond the urgent satisfaction of family needs or even of their own individual desires. Our present culture still strongly emphasises the importance of the individual over against the community. Baptismal policies should not strengthen this individualism by suggesting that baptism is only something done to the child, irrespective of the beliefs and practices of the parents, or the life of the local congregation. To imply this is to reinforce an atomised view of human, community and family life.

176   At the same time, not to allow for the proper, even if inarticulate, desire for baptism could also imply an individualism on the part of church members over against a concern being expressed in the wider community which needs to be affirmed. What is more, if evangelism is to be understood as 'not simply about recruiting new members to the Christian community, but being nothing less than the transformation of persons and situations' (para. 146) then it could be argued that those who have a 'restricted' baptismal policy are being too narrow in their restrictions if they limit them to a requirement of church attendance.

A proper tension

177   Undoubtedly the question of baptism faces the Church with a difficult choice. Should it, because of cultural and historical expectations, accept all who come and take the risk that a weak or confused faith will become stronger and clearer? Or should it challenge people to match their request with concrete evidence of an already committed faith, and risk misunderstanding and a feeling of alienation, which could be interpreted as denying the unmerited love of God? This choice is one which in fact is found wherever the Church has a deep concern for mission. Unless one advocates a complete split between the Gospel

and culture, between the Church and the world, the tension in this choice is inevitable. To take an uncompromising stance on either side could have serious consequences, either the stifling of God's activity in the world, or the removal of all costliness from the Gospel.

Chapter 11

WORSHIP IN DIFFERING CONTEXTS

178   In the epilogue to his book *The Church* Hans Küng says:

> There is basically nothing in the church which
> ought not to be done with windows open to
> the street – while concentrating on the work
> at hand, not simply staring out of the windows.

Some principles and some examples

179   'Religion' (as its derivation indicates) is supposed to *bind* all life
together. Worship is meant to be a sign or *sacrament* of that function.
In order that it may achieve that purpose there are two basic require-
ments:

Worship must accord with the Gospel. It must be recognisable as
Christian worship, recognisably within the tradition of the
Church's worship both in the past and in the present, in union
with the worship of the whole Church.

Worship must celebrate the day-to-day life of each particular local
congregation. It cannot be in a totally alienating language using
irrelevant symbols. It should celebrate not only the deeds that God
has done in the whole history of his people, but also those deeds
he is doing among us now.

In short, it must reflect the needs both of the local congregation and of
the whole church catholic. Only thus can it be authentic worship, no
matter who 'authorises' it.

180   Some of the main questions affecting culture and worship to which
answers are required would seem to be as follows:

(a) How to promote forms of worship adapted to different cultural groups yet at the same time preserving unity in Christ.

(b) How to ensure that the church is not worshipping in a sub-culture that is unnecessarily alienating from the wider society it is called to serve.

(c) How to identify vehicles (signs and symbols) that celebrate the spiritual experience of people who come to see that their experience may be associated with Christ.

(d) How to enable a congregation to celebrate the high and low points of their own life in the world.

(e) How to ensure a measure of freedom in worship so that each can use their gifts for the building up of the church.

Differing expectations
181 We can only move towards answers to such questions by looking at actual examples of worship, bearing in mind the different contexts for which each one was developed. People come to worship with varied expectations, often not clearly articulated even to themselves. For some, 'real' worship consists in reflection on the Scriptures leading to union with Christ. Others come to worship so that they might be united with Christ through the celebration of the sacraments. Some would like worship to consist in a withdrawal from the hustle of the world into a sacred space, going apart seeking spiritual strength before returning to the secular struggle. Some will come seeking quiet, help, forgiveness, security, merely for a reinforcement of their own beliefs, not wishing to be challenged.

182 We offer here some 'case studies' illustrating still further examples of expectations on the part either of the participants or the organisers (which unfortunately do not always coincide!).

'It was a sunny Sunday morning in May and the church was away on its annual houseparty. On a small table in the middle the children put the cross they had made, the clay they had moulded into a cup and a plate and the bread they had helped to bake. A bottle of wine and the elements were ready. In different corners readers prepared passages from Scripture, musicians prepared hymns and a group practised a specially adapted inclusive version of the Lord's Prayer. The liturgical group for the week composed prayers of intercession and thanksgiving and specially adapted the Prayer of Consecration for the occasion. Outside others put the finishing touches to the maypole around which they would sing "Lord of the Dance". Everybody had some contribution to make to the worship which would truly be "the work of the people". '

'The church was packed with a crowd of worshippers, some with arms in the air, others clapping hands, while one or two were dancing in the aisle. The music was modern and lively and the lyrics simple, with frequent repetition of key phrases. After the singing there was a variety of contributions from the congregation; some spoke in an unknown language (tongues); some shared a message from God (prophecy) while others had "words of knowledge" – "there is someone here with a chipped ankle bone". An invitation was given to come forward for healing, particularly those who had been identified by the words of knowledge. Some who had been standing collapsed in their seats (a phenomenon often described as being "slain in the Spirit").'

'When we received permission to admit all who were baptised to Holy Communion we agreed to disband the Sunday School and to exchange the "solo voiced sermon" for a one or two sentence teaching point which is then portrayed through drama. This work is undertaken by one of the four groups into which the congregation is divided. The drama is preceded by two choruses, one of which is likely to be an action song. We seek by this to open the heart by the use of the body. The prayers invite any to express their prayer to the prayer-leader during the hymn after the Creed. It is read out as the petitioner comes forward and lights a candle.'

'There are very few seats in our Orthodox church and the congregation stands for the most part, though individual members often walk about, visiting a favourite icon, lighting a candle, giving alms, or even going out for a break (after all, the liturgy does last for well over two hours). The priest moves in and out of the sanctuary, representing the Saviour Christ who comes from heaven to bring about the marriage of earth and heaven which God always intended. The congregation is caught up in this action in the glad song of the universe which the liturgy echoes. They join with the choir in all the singing because they have known the melodies and the harmonies since childhood. On some occasions, after serious preparation, they receive the most sacred Body and Blood of Jesus. At each liturgy they express their love for each other in their joint worship and in the bread of fellowship, pieces of which are taken to those who have not been able to be present.'

'My wife and I find that the 8 am Holy Communion service provides the quiet and reverent setting which we need to give our whole attention to God without distraction. As we were always taught, we read the Collect, Epistle and Gospel overnight. We rarely discuss the readings, believing preparation for receiving Our Lord in Communion to be a very private matter. We get up quietly and usually do not engage in ordinary conversation till we are back home at breakfast. Quite frankly we find chat with other members of the congregation before or after the service a real intrusion. The silence and the predictable, orderly liturgy helps us to ponder what has happened the previous week, bringing both thanksgiving and penitence, and to give ourselves for the coming week whatever it holds in store. Somehow we are united to each other, to our grown-up children and grandchildren, to those who have gone before us and to all church people in the silence of the prayer.'

Exploration of the issues

183   Worship should be the joyful celebration of life in the world. It should be our response to what we discover God to be doing in our lives. It must therefore relate the biblical message to our present situation. Our traditional celebrations have been of God's work in 'the history of our salvation' and also of the four major rites of passage: birth, coming of age, marriage and death. The *Alternative Service Book 1980*, the *American Book of Common Prayer* and the *Canadian Prayer Book* add blessings for some additional 'life experiences' – the adoption of a child, civil marriage, commitment to Christian service – but they still ignore many other significant moments of contemporary life. Other recently published liturgies can be found, centred on healing from contemporary ills such as violence, incest, wife-battering or rape, from distress on the occasion of an abortion, a burglary, or a divorce, as well as liturgies of celebration of a birthday, coming of age, cycles of earth and body. Through such liturgies the congregation can offer to God experiences which form part of the pattern of 'ordinary' life – or which have brutally interrupted that pattern for certain individuals in their midst.

> The congregation can offer to God experiences
> which form part of the pattern of 'ordinary' life
> – or which have brutally interrupted that pattern
> for certain individuals in their midst.

184   The Hillsborough football tragedy and the subsequent reaction of ordinary folk at Anfield was just one example of the urge people experience for a common, visible expression of their feelings. On this occasion there was a Roman Catholic Mass and other church observances. Two examples, during the Gulf War, were the increase in numbers watching 'Songs of Praise' and the newspaper photographs of army chaplains standing behind makeshift altars in the desert. But too often the church's worship is out of touch with current events, either not recognising them as occasions when God is touching us or by offering worship in a language and form that is quite alien to present society. It would be absurd to suggest that every liturgical act should embrace the whole range of faith and of our experience but there is a need for local celebrations of local experiences that the Christian Church should seek to penetrate with understanding and then bring before God in appropriate worship. Unfortunately this does not always happen. One of us recalls a visit made by a group to the North East of England. 'During the day we travelled the area seeing the devastation wrought by industrial decay and mass unemployment. In our morning and evening worship I found myself unable to sing – questioning the relevance of the language and concepts in the hymns to the experience of the people we had been visiting.'

185   Worship can in some groups become purely an emotional trip, concerned only with giving free play to devotional feelings. This can be a form of escapism, the worship of a group separated from the life of the world. Even more formal congregations often seem to be happy with a worship that deliberately seeks to be different from what goes on 'in the world'. There are, of course, many churches which, in varying degrees, struggle to avoid any total retreat into 'Church culture' and to stay open to the world. They seek to relate worship and life experience and to keep the door open to those who want to come in. The danger here can be that worship is made so much a thing of this life, so much linked in with contemporary society, so much adapted to cultural values that it adopts a purely secularist view, failing to challenge contemporary values with those of the Gospel. The congregation

becomes merely one social group worshipping in itself, but losing sight of God's transcendence.

The problem with 'local' forms
186 In the situation where a basic religious sense conflicts with secularist assumptions worship is inevitably a place where conflicting cultures meet, and it would be wrong to seek to avoid the reality of this clash of cultures simply by perpetuating unnecessary cultural barriers. Even in this situation we need to accept that worship ought to be *indigenous* and not transplanted from an alien or foreign culture.

> Youth culture and octogenarian culture, Asian, West Indian, Cockney — what is meaningful for one may not be equally so for others

187 However, the problem is that there are many cultures and subcultures in our society – youth culture and octogenarian culture, Asian, West Indian, Cockney. What is meaningful for one may not be equally so for the others. Many immigrant Christians have found British worship staid and apparently cold and unfriendly. Some cultural forms can threaten those of another background. The kiss of peace can threaten some and can seem constrained to others. The music, the forms of prayer, the words, the bodily reactions all will be cultural. God comes to us in our bodies in different ways. How are we to celebrate sacraments which unite the material and spiritual in a way that speaks to these different perceptions? Corporate worship requires sharing.

188 Of course, it is easier to share experiences within smaller, more homogeneous groups (see further paras 216f) and perhaps in some congregations there may be a need to question the strong emphasis placed on 'The Parish Communion'. There is need to balance the formal with the personal. The church needs to free its worship so that there is more creativity, relevance and participation. But equally there is need to balance the small-group experience with the experience of the wider and more diverse congregation. What is more, we are members not only of the local congregation but of the whole world church. The task of the kingdom in the service of others requires that our worship be as inclusive as possible, enriched by the experience of many.

Maintaining the wider reference

> Worship must accord with the doctrine of the
> Church

189 An awareness of the whole world-wide church, and the recognition that worship is the common possession of the whole people of God, that the church is one will mean that patterns and forms cannot be solely at the whim of a local congregation. Creeds, collects, confessions, eucharist prayers, must bear witness to the wider life of the church. There are of course many traditions within the Anglican Communion, but within all of them the worship must accord with the doctrine of the church. Perhaps the best way forward is the indication of structures, patterns and forms which also allow for adaptation and experiment, as has been done in *Patterns for Worship* (Liturgical Commission. 1990).

190 Even though most people lack liturgical education and there will be need for relatively simple explanation of the sources of liturgical form, the underlying theology, and the safeguards necessary, different congregations should be able, within the given framework, specifically to reflect their own tradition and culture. Some will be more evangelistic, some more cerebral, some more socially and politically involved, some more pentecostal, some more liberal, some more traditional, none exclusive, all related to their local cultural setting. Different situations will permit of varying degrees of creativity. In areas where there have been relatively few clergy there has already been much lay creativity and participation and these experiences can become models.

Younger members at worship
191 A 'sub-culture' with which the Church is in constant, if somewhat puzzled, contact consists of its own younger members. How can these young people be helped to see the significance of the Church's worship for them? They need to be helped to understand that, though worship appears to be for the middle aged and elderly, it need not be so.

192 For this to happen there needs to be adjustment on both sides. As we have seen, the worship we do in church is the celebration of the link between Christians throughout the world and throughout history; back to Jesus of Nazareth and forward to the end of time. But it also needs

to be readily accessible and immediate. When young people are carried by a feeling or belief, they want to act on it now, and not at some indefinite point in the future. Prayers need to be specific, and urgent, pouring out from the heart as well as the mind. Young people need to worship in a way that is pared down of wordiness and of excessive intellectualism, but is honest with emotions. Consideration will need to be given to the involvement of young people in the planning and preparation of services, and to styles of music and the use of language.

Forms and symbols

Eucharistic prayers – creeds, or thanksgivings?

193　Alongside the problem of somehow finding meeting points between youth culture and liturgy there are far more radical questions that can be asked about forms and language of worship. Our Eucharistic Prayers derive for the most part from fifth-century patterns and are couched in terms of redemption and atonement well suited to that age. They tend to be creed-like rather than acts of thanksgiving. Perhaps other images might be more apt for different groups – images of covenant proclamation, of thanksgiving, of a common meal, of divine forgiveness. There have been some experimental Eucharistic Prayers written for India, Kenya, and Zaire. Are those suggested for use in contemporary England in *Patterns for Worship* sufficiently radical to be effective?

194　For her own sake, as well as for the sake of her mission, the Church needs to seek for and to identify vehicles (signs and symbols) suited to the celebration of the spiritual experiences of those outside her boundaries. She needs to look within contemporary culture for the symbols of grief, of joy, of reaching beyond that are apt for her. The Church should seek to build on those vehicles which others use to handle their more significant experiences. She needs also to re-interpret her own symbols so that she can both acquire and offer new and deeper insights into contemporary culture. In this way the Living God can bring new life both to the Church and to the community at large.

Worship for the community

195　The Church has community at its heart and generates community beyond its worshipping boundaries. Others may be attracted by this, though there might still be a wide gap between glimpsing this fact and actually coming to share in worship. The greatest opportunities arise where church and local community share tasks and hopes. The key to this often comes from the Christian recognition that where you touch the poor you are touching Christ. One example of where Church and community have set out to cross the cultural boundaries between them in a positive and creative way is provided by St Paul's, Deptford. Canon David Diamond has been Rector for some 20 years. He came to a run-down eighteenth-century building. He restored the building to be, in John Betjeman's words, 'a pearl in the heart of Deptford'. More importantly, he had the vision of a vibrant, confident, open community life which keeps people in the Borough around aware of what the church offers. At times in his ministry this aim has been brilliantly achieved. In a brochure to mark the 250th year of the building Canon Diamond quotes *Faith in the City*: '... what we must move towards is a church which is rooted locally, which expresses the culture of the locality, which reacts, interacts, with that culture and therefore with the people and the life-style of those people who surround it'. The brochure is full of lively 'people' pictures and enthusiastic awareness of how life is for ordinary people.

196   In a covering letter with the brochure Canon Diamond wrote that he had found the traditional presentation of the Mass the ideal instrument for bringing such diversity as they had in Deptford together. A cerebral act of worship would tend to divide, but the Mass was capable of bringing very different people together in a common experience of adoration. The Mass is the especial crown of the annual Deptford Festival.

'But it is not just the Festival that begins and ends at the altar – everything must. Here on the altar we offer not only all the sorrows and tragedies of Deptford life (and there are plenty of these) but the joys and the celebrations of the community too. Here it is that God takes these lowly things, changes and transforms them into the risen and glorified life of Jesus – so that his transforming power can be taken into the life of the community again. 10.30 am each Sunday and 6 pm each weekday sees this wondrous exchange between Deptford and Heaven and nothing can be so important as this.'

Examples are then given of police and angry black people at Mass together at a time of imminent riot, and of the football team and supporters at a time of tension. The final picture we are left with is that of a massed school choir with Jamaicans, Nigerians, Asians, Pakistanis, Turkish-Cypriots, Indians – 'yes, and Irish-Cockneys too!'

197 David Diamond's vision has been shared by countless parish priests and faithful Christians who believe that what they do in church they do for all. Christ has died and is alive not only for the few but for the whole new humanity and the Church exists to encourage all to find that truth and their home in God. Such Christians bring the life around them into the Mass, the material stuff which bread and wine symbolise. They bring it all into the saving plan of God lived out in Christ who died and rose again, setting free new power of the Holy Spirit into the world. Some have had the resources and imagination to get their vision across to a locality in a way which has brought people with very varying degrees of comprehension to be caught up into an atmosphere of celebration and community-belongingness in a mode totally congruous with the culture around them. The liturgy of the Mass may not be understood, but the feeling of what it is about communicates. This is the heart of catholic life and evangelism, the infectious non-cerebral impact which leads on to deepening by other means.

198 Paramount among the many and complex themes we have tried to cover in this chapter is the necessity of finding a balance between understanding and experience. If the language of worship is immediately accessible to all, it is likely to be superficial. Moreover, Christian worship will always challenge accepted values. Any group which seeks to challenge the values of the culture around them will need to create some marks of distinction between 'them' and 'us'. Conventions are necessary and a learning process is involved for all those who wish to participate. But the Christian congregation must never be closed in on itself. It must be neither exclusive nor escapist. It must seek to ensure that in its worship, as in the rest of its activity, it is being true to the authentic Gospel.

Chapter 12

CHURCH STRUCTURES AS VEHICLES OF THE GOSPEL

A case study and *Faith in the City*

199 Chester-le-Street is a town of about 30,000 inhabitants, half-way between Durham and Newcastle. Christian worship on the site of its ancient parish church dates back to AD 883. In the nighteenth century the town became ringed with mining villages and the parish church established 'mission' churches within them. After the Second World War the pits began to close, the villages declined and the mission churches were no longer viable. However, the town remained a strategic communications centre in the North East, the population eventually began to grow again and new estates sprang up which had no visible corporate Christian witness. The parish responded by establishing area congregations on the estates. Growth took place on a 'strawberry plant' principle. Members of the parish church who were resident in a neighbourhood established new 'plants' or community churches which rooted themselves at a distance from the 'parent' church. At first the new plants were heavily dependent on the parent, but eventually they established a semi-autonomous life of their own.[16]

200 These developments illustrate a number of the issues we have already been examining. The new congregations met in what was for them familiar rather than alienating settings – in schools, clubs and even a pub. The church was perceived therefore as coming to the people rather than as an elite group associated with the distant parish church building. Local leadership and a high level of local participation were encouraged, ensuring that the life and worship of the congregations matched the culture of the area. The principle of uniformity in worship throughout the parish was abandoned and local accents were to be heard in leadership of services while intercessions began to reflect the concerns of the local community. These concerns were also met by practical responses. As well as witnessing through the provision of welcome evenings and courses in basic Christianity the area churches were instrumental in the setting up of a play group, youth clubs and a keep fit class, and a scheme to provide domiciliary care for the terminally ill. In other words the overall strategy was community based

rather than church based, with the emphasis on finding the right structures for evangelism rather than simply concentrating on the methods.

> Commitment to what is local in patterns of worship, music, presentation of the Gospel and theology

201 *Faith in the City* (1985) argued that churches in Urban Priority Areas needed to become 'local, outward-looking, participating and ecumenical' (ch. 4.7). *Local* churches must be committed to the local community and neighbourhood. This includes commitment to what is local in patterns of worship, music, presentation of the Gospel and theology. They must also be sensitive to local cultures and local life-styles in leadership and manner of operating (ch. 4.10). Church organisation and committee structures need to be appropriate. The use of formal committees, agendas and minutes could de-skill those from a non-literate culture and result in central church organisations becoming dominated by those from a middle class culture.

202 An *outward-looking* church is one that believes that God is at work in the world around and not just in the Church (ch. 4.15). This leads to both *participating* in local life and *ecumenical* partnership with others. Some argue therefore that in our modern urban context the parochial system itself is outdated and inappropriate. *Faith in the City* (ch. 5), however, argues that what is needed is not a radical scrapping, but development and sometimes reorganisation. We attempt to deal in detail with various aspects of these issues in the following paragraphs.

Parish boundaries

> Mission is what the Triune God does in the world to bring humankind to wholeness

203 The Church, it has been said, is only the Church when it is in mission. We understand 'mission' to be what the Triune God does in the world to bring humankind to wholeness. The Church is called to be an agent of this divine action, both identifying where it is taking place and seeking to reinforce it, and offering itself as a channel for its

functioning, where the divine action is otherwise hindered. The building up of the inner life of the Church only has full meaning when its purpose is to look and serve beyond its own boundaries. As we have argued elsewhere in this report, growth is properly a process of development towards maturity and not solely a development in size. How much restructuring and how much rearranging within existing structures this requires is a matter for serious debate.

204 When most people think of the Church of England they probably first have the vicar or parson in mind, then the parish church. If they want to get married in a particular parish church, they will have to find out in which parish they live because that dictates in which churches they may legally be married. It will be unfortunate for their plans if they live on the wrong side of the street. Anglican parish boundaries are reasonably comprehensible in the countryside, although they sometimes follow bridleways rather than modern roads, but they do not make obvious sense in towns and cities.

205 The organisational structures of the Church of England appear rural not only in their origins but in their continuing assumptions. There are still *rural* deans in many sizeable cities, even though the title 'Area Dean' has been substituted in some dioceses in the last couple of decades. In a society organised around small village communities, with a tradition of hierarchical structures, the parochial system made a good deal of sense. The parson was the representative *person* of the Church. Along with the building he *was* the Church. Whatever its historical appropriateness, the question now is whether the parochial system is any longer relevant other than in the countryside.

The urban context
206 Away from the context of a rural society parish boundaries seem to have less obvious relevance. In every highly populated conurbation local Christians pass each other on their way to worship at different churches, exercising their consumer's right of choice. Moreover, the old concept of the parson as *the* representative of the Church in *the* community simply does not transfer to the modern urban scene. Society itself is more democratic and communitarian. This factor has coincided with the Church's realisation, following the New Testament precedent of shared ministry, that there is need to develop local recognition of a representative *group* of people, the Christian community, the Body of Christ or the People of God.

'Parson' and People committed to the local community and not just to themselves

207 Nevertheless, urban churches have often found parish boundaries still to be a helpful way of establishing a territory within which they are responsible for exercising pastoral care. Rightly used they can help to ensure that 'parson' *and* people are committed to the local community and not just to themselves. The function of a boundary is to make a situation manageable, in other words to try to provide some order out of chaos. Barbed wire fences around defence establishments are there to keep people out. There are high walls around prisons to keep people in. However, heat exchangers, which are also boundaries, exist in order to enable heat to pass from one area to another. Similarly the walls of a womb are boundaries which enable nurture to pass from the mother's body to her unborn child.

208 Can parish boundaries be used in this way so that one church can nurture another? In some areas there may be one or more flourishing churches among several struggling ones. One approach is to form a group or team of clergy. Another is to encourage the flourishing church to 'transplant' members of their congregation into a struggling church. A third approach is to 'church-plant', establishing a completely new congregation in the area, as happened in Chester-le-Street. Church-planting may be attempted in the same parish as the parent church or in a different one. In both cases the approval of the bishop and the goodwill of other churches in the district will obviously be needed, but this is particularly so if the 'plant' takes place across a parish boundary.

Problems of alternative approaches
209 Group and team ministries have many advantages, but also one or two difficulties. By and large clergy are not trained for team ministry, and without very great care the larger the group or team of clergy the more the laity can feel excluded. All three approaches can raise cross-cultural issues, especially if the area is not a monochrome one. Some 'flourishing' churches only flourish because they are homogeneous units, able to appeal to a particular section of the population and creaming off the skilled or gifted members from parishes around. In such a case 'church planting' would be more accurately described as 'recycling'. Furthermore, if church planting is undertaken with a team

from a different culture than that of the local church or community there is danger that the skills of those from the local community will be overlooked or ignored. On the other hand there are several cases of successful church planting where these problems have not occurred and if the flourishing church is outward looking, sensitive and humble it can provide valuable training facilities that are not available to weaker churches. The more that mutual sharing can take place across parish boundaries the better for the health of the churches in the area.

> 'How to choose a satisfactory church'

210   While there are problems with the geographical basis of the parish system there are also dangers with any alternative system of networks. As we shall see in a moment, these can too easily become merely groups of like-minded individuals. Its members may unconsciously adopt the philosophy and methods of the consumer society, seeking 'satisfaction' from their church life as they would from any other commodity. Indeed, the first chapter in one American Episcopalian book on 'Mutual Ministry' is on 'How to choose a satisfactory church'. In contrast, the ancient parochial system of the Church of England (and of the Presbyterian Established Church of Scotland) is concerned to provide Christian ministry within the whole of a locality. It is concerned with ministry to a community, not just to those individuals within it who claim to belong to the Anglican Church. Perhaps the best way forward is to modify rather than dismantle the parochial system and at the same time to encourage the further development of *additional* networks, especially within education and industry and among ethnic and other groups. Industrial and community chaplaincies are already well established in some areas, as a complement to the underlying parochial system.

Other partners in the system
211   Many Free Churches are equally concerned with ministry to the surrounding community and not just to their own members. This is especially significant at a time when a number of Anglican churches appear to be under pressure to concentrate primarily on serving the needs of their own congregations. If what have traditionally been known as 'gathered' churches are more and more concerned with serving their neighbours in the world around them, there is all the more

reason for re-emphasising what the proper priorities for *any* church ought to be. One of the many memorable sayings of William Temple was that the Church was the only body that existed primarily for the sake of those who were not its members. Therefore it is desirable that the Church of England should consult with other churches at local level as to what the future of the parochial system needs to be. There is one way in which adaptation has already begun, in the setting up of Local Ecumenical Projects (see further paras 272/3). The experience gained from these 'first-fruits' needs to be used to provide the vision for a more general adaptation of the parochial system in co-operation with other churches. What better time is there for this task than the 1990s with the birth in hope of the new ecumenical instruments?

212   In many towns and cities the quite distinct cultures which different churches have developed out of their varied histories enrich each other's members and provide them with new visions of Christian discipleship. If the parochial system were to be dismantled, as distinct from being rationalised, what would be the best alternatives for rural, suburban and urban areas, having regard to the many local cultures involved? In the United Reformed Church some have dreamed of 'ecumenical mission deaneries' across the country as a way of getting unity in mission at the ground level. In the Church of England there has been for a few years an informal Deaneries Group attempting to stimulate thinking about how the deanery could best be developed as a unit for mission. Should this group be encouraged to become ecumenical in its thinking and membership? At present the deanery is seen as a peculiarly Anglican concern, even though the Roman Catholic Church also has a deanery structure.

213   Then again, how should the Church share its thinking about this issue with other community organisations, statutory and voluntary, both to learn from them and to share with them its long and widespread experience? It should discuss with the residents and with local organisations the ways in which the inheritance of the past needs to be adapted for the future, and how the Church's aspiration to foster *worship, nurture* and *mission* in a wide variety of neighbourhoods would best fit in with the needs and cultures of local residents as they perceive them.

Practical steps forward

> Many parishes have made progress through
> shared ministry schemes, by mission audits and
> by learning business-like planning methods

214   Often it is assumed that large decisions involving legislation need to be achieved before any progress along these lines can be made. This sometimes appears to be used as a kind of alibi to postpone the type of helpful change that could in fact be made without legislation. Many parishes have made progress through shared ministry schemes and mission audits and by learning business-like planning methods. They have made progress by achieving a little at a time. The key to progress concerning boundaries and appropriate mission and ministry development is of course not only the local clergy but the bishops and their diocesan advisers. We shall return to this issue in the next chapter.

215   Mention was made in para. 210 of the dangers inherent in small 'like-minded' congregations. What can be done when the whole population in an area shares very much the same characteristics and this is inevitably reflected in the congregation? One answer is to provide cross-cultural fellowship at deanery or diocesan level or to explore the possibility of 'twinning'. In the city of Bristol, for example, deanery boundaries have been deliberately planned like spokes of a wheel in order to link inner city, urban and rural areas. The experience of UPA churches is now beginning to highlight the issues which suburban churches need to deal with as they face a changing future. Where the necessary coming and going between UPA and other parishes is not possible within a deanery basis, much can be achieved through twinning arrangements, either between individual parishes or in some cases by dioceses. A number of such schemes have successfully been set up as a result of demand, despite initial discouragement from the Follow Up Advisory Group of the Archbishops' Commission on Urban Priority Areas.

Homogeneous groups
216   The need to achieve a proper cross-cultural 'mix', is not, however, the only consideration to be borne in mind. At several points in this report we have stressed the need to provide a Christian community or

fellowship that can give and preserve a sense of identity for those who belong – whether or a black-led church or Asian Christian fellowship. Such fellowships are sometimes described as *homogeneous* units, because those who belong are of one race, class or kind. The concept, if not the term, is a common one. There may be congregations of one social class either in an affluent part of suburbia or on a monochrome housing estate. Even at the same parish church there may be three separate congregations, divided by taste if not by culture, coming to BCP Communion at 8, to Rite A Family Eucharist at 9.30 and to Sung Matins or High Mass at 11. In a former age it was traditional for the gentry to worship in the morning and the servants in the evening; if they did come to the same service the system of pew rents kept social mixing within bounds.

217 In certain circumstances homogeneity may be both unavoidable and unfortunate. In other circumstances it may prove to be a necessary and *positive* characteristic of part of a church's structures. While one of the key marks of the Church is 'catholicity' and the ultimate aim is to create a fellowship that embraces all ages, languages, races and cultures, there are sometimes practical arguments for a number of homogeneous units to be created *within* a parish. There is a case for providing such units for youth, young parents or senior citizens to enable them to share their particular concerns and interests.

218 With young people there are additional reasons for adopting such an approach. One of the most common features of teenage life and beyond is a *need* to get together in small groups. Safety comes from the smallness of the group and the mutual loyalty that can only be engendered at that level. We need to encourage young people in their small groups, even allowing for regular worship within those small groups, and providing material for easily accessible Bible work.

> It takes a lot of courage for a young person to opt for faith, let alone choose the Church of England

219 The Church has to acknowledge that it takes a lot of courage today for a young person to opt for faith, let alone choose the Church of England. Schools, colleges, pubs and clubs can be harsh places of quiet

persecution for the confessing Christian, and we need to spend far more of our time, our money, our imagination and our prayers on the task of making the gospel a visible and audible option in life for the young. We will need to put more young people in visible positions of responsibility and power within the Church, so that they can be the role models for others to work towards. We need to encourage in this way not just the perfect, either, but all those who have expressed their commitment, with whatever level of 'spiritual success', so that they can grow and flourish, not as 'honorary adults', but as young people valued for their very youth.

Ethnically-based sub-groups
220 Similarly, if Asian members of a congregation are in a minority, there is value in providing opportunity for study and worship in their own Asian language and in ensuring that the rich heritage of their culture is not swamped by the dominant culture of the congregation at large. There is a vast variety of Christian minority groups both in this country and overseas. Of the Asian people living in Britain only a small minority are Christians, so they are a minority within a minority. There are also many groups from various countries in Africa. In all these cases there seems to be a need for some form of separate life which goes hand in hand with any attempt at integration. In the case of some of the Asians and those from Africa this takes the form of chaplaincies which combine social with religious needs. In England there are, for example, chaplaincies for Chinese and Japanese Christians, and similar chaplaincies for Ghanaians and Nigerians.

> There seems to be the need for some form of separate life which goes hand in hand with any attempt at integration

221 The history of Afro-Caribbean immigrants has been different. They are part of a Christian *majority* who have come to Britain in a movement of population which has been called 'colonialisation in reverse'. As a result, as we noted in Chapter 3, they have tended to form their own separate churches. Many, however, have remained within the mainline churches and, in recent years, have formed organisations to build up their sense of identity as Black Christians, loyal to their culture and way of expressing their faith in worship, theology and social

concern, as well as to the wider Church. Apart from such groups as exist at the local level, there is 'The Association of Black Clergy' and 'The Black Ecumenical Youth Association'. Both of these started as Anglican organisations but are now ecumenical. 'Claiming the Inheritance' was ecumenical from the beginning, as was 'The Black and White Christian Partnership' based at Selly Oak. From the purely Anglican perspective, there is the General Synod's 'Committee for Black Anglican Concerns', while a number of dioceses have their own committees and, occasionally, officers for such affairs.

222 The acts of worship as well as the other activities devised for and created by these groups should be drawn from cultural forms familiar to the members of each unit. This, however, could carry the risk of disunity. There is always the danger that a small group will seek to protect itself and erect barriers that exclude the stranger, and to counteract this danger we would suggest one possible model for consideration. Group worship could be supplemented by a coming together of all units from time to time, say once a quarter, to manifest and increase their unity in Christ. On such occasions the resultant large congregation would not consist of so many individuals but of so many *groups*, and each person would be participating in a common act of worship in virtue of his/her group membership.

223 The best of cultural heritage should be preserved and transformed through homogeneous groups not just for its own sake but so that those from other backgrounds can be enriched. It is significant that one of the tasks of the Japanese chaplain referred to above is to encourage Japanese Christians to integrate into local churches. Some parishes have a structure that balances 'cross-cultural' worship and *mixed* house groups with homogeneous units for youth or senior citizens. In North America it has become increasingly common to plan one major worship time for all each week, followed by 'all-age Sunday school' teaching in appropriate groups.

Maintaining a 'norm'
224 Whenever adults combine in groups, for whatever reason, each group needs to be small enough for its members to know and trust each other, but all the relevant groups need to be linked together in the sort of networks necessary to provide coherence of congregational life. This is particularly true for those in UPAs, but the implications also ring true for churches in middle class and in rural areas.

225 The establishment of homogeneous groups is equally important for those on the fringe of church life. The worship designed for youth in the Coventry area (see para. 57) would not have been acceptable in a traditional congregation. This sometimes works in the opposite direction. Some of those recruited to the 'church-in-a-pub' in Chester-le-Street (para. 200) found the location a barrier to full participation. Their previous, though minimal, experience of church culture demanded a more traditional setting for worship.

Groups and evangelism

> Homogeneous units can only ever be justified as 'staging-posts' towards a fellowship that is fully 'catholic'

226 For purposes of direct evangelism the homogeneous unit can also be very effective. Some of the more extreme teaching about church growth has argued for maintaining complete and continuing homogeneity of small groups, on the grounds that this leads to the fastest growth. It is argued that many people reject the gospel not because they think it false, but because it seems alien, and that it is easier for people to respond to the gospel if they do not have to cross racial, linguistic or class barriers to do so. But homogeneous units can only ever be justified as *staging posts* towards a fellowship that is fully 'catholic'. Indeed such a wider fellowship may in itself be an effective witness to the gospel, even to the newcomer, acting as a showcase for the harmony of the kingdom. The New Testament contains evidence of different groupings on cultural lines in the early church. Acts 6 speaks of 'Hellenists' and 'Hebrews' and it is significant that those set apart to look after the needs of Hellenists were probably from the same background. Yet there is nothing to suggest that this was a permanent arrangement or that there was any scheme of 'separate development'.

227 Almost all involved in direct evangelism through parishes affirm the value of neighbourhood groups. Ernest Southcott in the Sixties spoke of intensive and extensive groups. *Extensive* groups are where more than half the participants are non-churchgoers. Such groups, often set up in 'parish missions' or in special evangelistic periods in a parish, require churchgoers to be sufficiently in touch with and trusted

by their neighbours so that they can invite them to coffee, tea or supper, 'followed by a serious discussion', and the invitation be accepted. With a catalyst to set it going, people can be encouraged to share their stories and with them their questions, their doubts, resentments, hurts, etc in an atmosphere where it is safe and they will be listened to. Inherent faith in God is often included in such sharing and can lead on to more explicit questions and expression of belief. Experience shows with what delight non-churchgoing people (once they have lost their terror) welcome a listening, accepting church, and with what delight churchgoing people (once they have lost their terror) find they can share with others their hopes and fears about God and learn from others.

Chapter 13

LEADERSHIP AND CULTURAL CHANGE

Patterns of leadership

228 When a new vicar is inducted after a vacancy in a parish the churchwardens and PCC often heave a great sigh of relief and say that the new incumbent will now *take over the leadership* of the church. Sometimes he is only too happy to feel that he is needed, and so priest and people collude with each other. They depend on him and he depend on them to need him. There are, however, many new examples of group leadership in which clergy (including women deacons) and lay people work together in pastoral care, mission and concern for the wider community.

229 But the danger still remains that the vicar may have been given answers and methods during his college training which do not fit the context of many parishes today. He may be sent out lacking many of the necessary skills, including the insights of community development. The incumbent may do too much himself and overwork his 'core group' who then collude with his model of leadership and distance themselves from their own colleagues. The tendency is for this strong group to repress the activity of the rest of the church membership without recognising what they are doing. They then blame the majority for being apathetic.

> Leadership styles are influenced by our context and culture

230 As with other aspects of church life, leadership styles are influenced by our context and culture. This was true in both Old and New Testament days. Unfortunately some styles persist long after the cultural context has altered. It can be argued that the episcopal organisation of the Church of England was, and still is, the ecclesiastical equivalent of the feudal system.

The 'professional' model
231 In modern western society there is always the danger that the priest may be tempted to follow the model of the contemporary *professional*. He has often been bracketed in the public mind with the doctor, architect and research scientist, possessing a mysterious expertise, special status and technical language that sets him apart from the non-professional or 'lay' person. Some have criticised traditional training for priesthood as taking place in a kind of theological Sandhurst, producing an elitist officer class that is distanced from other ranks. Even those who hold leadership positions in industry or the community tend to feel themselves de-skilled when they enter through the church door. Captains of industry are harnessed to hand out hymn books. Even though Jesus was incarnated into first century Palestine culture He refused to follow the authoritarian styles of leadership in contemporary society. 'You know that the men who are considered rulers of the heathen have power over them and the leaders have complete authority. This is not the way it is among you. If one of you wants to be great, he must be the servant of the rest' (Mark 10.42f). He was concerned to identify with the powerless, rather than exercise power through special status or authority.

A new approach needed
232 In trying to develop appropriate patterns of leadership today a change of heart on the part of both clergy and lay people is necessary. It requires a *proper* professionalism on the part of the clergy, involving a deliberate decision to trust others whatever the risk. 'Vicar, you've done yourself out of a job', said a churchwarden to an incumbent who had tried to share responsibility. This was true in one sense, but he had also rediscovered another job – to be the one who assists the people to work at the real needs of their own situation, the one who can be consulted, who can ask the sharp questions. He sought the educational skills gently to foster and elicit the skills and devotion of the people of God.

> Lay people can be empowered, not inhibited,
> affirmed, not de-skilled

233 In this way lay people can be empowered not inhibited, affirmed not de-skilled. But this involves a 'change of heart' on their part as well. There is an urgent need to deal with the feelings on the part of many

lay people that they can bring nothing useful to their church membership other than their mere presence at worship. Affirming people
means a willingness to consult them in such a way that they feel their
opinion is being taken seriously.

Leadership in UPAs

234 Developing indigenous leadership in urban priority and other
areas can mean a lengthy process of patient encouragement. Individuals gain confidence and support by working as a team. Some UPA
parishes have encouraged the members of house groups to plan and
lead worship so encouraging group rather than solo leadership. In this
way hidden talents are unearthed. One parish has learnt to use support
groups (rather than committees) for teaching and worship. Clergy who
recognise that others have greater skills in using informal language in
liturgical settings may gratefully encourage lay leadership in, for instance, Eucharistic intercessions or more generally in 'family services'.
Most British clergy, however, believe that the overall responsibility for
worship remains with them.

235 Total involvement of the laity in this way is, of course, not *just* an
approach appropriate only to certain sub-cultures. Reflection on what
we have identified as 'Signs of Authenticity' (para. 84) will suggest that
very few Christians have yet discovered ways in which the Gospel may
become concrete in the building of new communities which both rejoice
in the grace of God and display signs of the reversal of a broken and
corrupt order in the power of the Spirit. Experience in the Base Ecclesial
Communities which have sprung up throughout Latin America indicates that such communities must be trusted to develop their own style
of life, worship and leadership as the members search the Scriptures
for themselves, listen to God in prayer and worship and continue to be
sensitive to the pains and struggles of the people around them and in
their midst. This means that the professional leadership of the existing
churches (whether clerical or lay) hands over effective control to the
groups themselves.

236 In these circumstances the priest will be consultant rather than
manager and the leaders will be local, thrown up from within and below
rather than imposed from outside and above. As such they are unlikely
to impose styles of leadership, language and learning that are foreign
to the group. Their agenda will deal with drains as well as doctrine,
with the need for decent housing as well as spirituality. One example

from Latin America is 'The community of hope', based in a Brazilian shanty town, that has as its four priorities – catechesis (popular Christian education), health, housing and prayer.

Lessons from the Black Churches
237 Another important example, from much nearer home, is the experience of the Afro-Caribbean communities in this country. This experience, whether nurtured within the historic or the black-led churches, has a contribution to make within the English context, not only in terms of reflecting on what they have known by way of suffering and rejection (which is now to a great extent also their lot in Britain), but also in sharing what they have to offer by way of flexibility and sheer joy in *worship*, of *patterns of shared leadership and ministry* and of appropriate forms of *training for leadership*.

238 One of the strengths of the black-led churches is that with them leadership does indeed come from the people. They understand the meaning of *non-stipendiary* ('tent-making') *ministry* and the reality of *shared ministry*, which enables lay people, male and female, to participate in *proclamation and presidency*. From them we in the historic churches have much to learn about the Church as institution and as communion.[17] There is a shared experience, including that of shared rejection and suffering, between leader and led.

239 It is often argued by some from the dominant culture and historic churches that there is a lack of theological coherence and an emphasis on biblical fundamentalism in black-led churches, which arises precisely *from* their forms of shared ministry. But such arguments may be rebutted by the assertion that biblical fundamentalism is different from biblical literalism. There is a proper place for biblical fundamentalism where the biblical text is allowed to speak directly to our context. Another charge is that the black-led churches lay too much emphasis on individual salvation and a privatised gospel. But those who make this charge fail to notice the social dynamics and interdependence of the black-led Christian community and its awareness of its place within the total structure (including the political) of society. The liberative force of the Gospel leads to social engagement in education, social work and politics.

Encouraging lay-leadership

240 Too often it is assumed in the historic churches that there is no leadership material within particular congregations. There are many parishes where skilful training by clergy and professional leaders has disproved this assertion. For example, it has been shown that many of the best people to work with the young are other young people. Experience with 'Time for God' and other similar initiatives suggests that the Church ought to employ a lot more young people quite specifically to engage in the business of spreading the news of God's love. Parishes as well as deaneries need to consider taking on school-leavers, training them in the faith, and employing them to work exclusively with the young. After all, in the Bible it is they who are expected to dream dreams, they whom Jesus wants close to him, they in whom God constantly puts his trust. So there is a need to train them in self-confidence, whilst being wary of removing them from contact with their friends.

> ... consider taking on school leavers, training
> them in their faith and empowering them
> to work exclusively with the young

241 It is not only the young that have tended to be neglected by the Church as potential leaders. Even where a strong tradition of lay involvement has been established it always seems so much easier to turn to those who already have well-developed educational skills. Such an attitude, however, robs the Church of potential new strengths. There are certain principles which need to be observed when people 'who can read, but don't' are trained for leadership. These include the need to use *stories* about concrete situations, whether about themselves, the local church or the local community around it. In addition it is necessary to train people in *groups;* the New Testament picture is of 'ordinary' people being taught skills of loving, caring and theological reflection through *experience,* followed by *review* and *reflection. Language* also needs to be kept simple, avoiding the use of the 'in language' that is too often developed by professional people and church people.

242 One example which takes these principles seriously is the *Group for Urban Ministry and Leadership (GUML),* set up in Liverpool in 1984 and described in *The Measure of Mission* (1987).[18] This scheme is con-

cerned to enable lay people to accept and exercise responsibility and power so that they can participate fully in the process of church life. It has a mandate from the Liverpool Diocesan Synod to select and train ministerial teams in UPA parishes and further to train some individuals for Local Non-Stipendiary Ministry. The Vicar has to be a member of the training group and agree to share his responsibility with it. It is said he has to sign away his autonomy.

> Group-training gives people power to grow in confidence and to be articulate about what they think is important

By 1989 there were 14 teams, almost equally women and men, whose members were engaged in a variety of ministries, such as bereavement counselling, baptism preparation and evangelism. Experience has shown that this style of group-training gives people power to grow in confidence and to be articulate about what they think is important. Nevertheless not everything has gone smoothly. There are signs of conflict within some of the teams and sometimes a new incumbent has had difficulty in accepting the joint leadership pattern.

The Cure of Souls

243   One source of such difficulties may well be an incumbent's understanding of the concept of *The Cure of Souls*. This is the legal term through which authority and responsibility for the well-being of all residents within the geographical limits of a parish is conferred. In the legal ceremony of Institution this is given to a priest by the bishop, who accepts him as a colleague with the words 'Receive this cure, which is mine and thine'. It is the bestowing of the 'spiritualities' of a benefice. The 'temporalities' – the property and financial endowments – are bestowed by the archdeacon through the 'Induction'. This latter is a distinct legal ceremony, even though now normally held at the same service as the Institution. Both *spiritualities* and *temporalities* are forms of property conferred as a freehold or leasehold, and together are what provides an incumbent, as opposed to a priest-in-charge, with spiritual responsibilities and financial support through endowment. The concept has deep emotional implications for the clergy and constitutes the geographical areas within which residents have the right to call on the services of the Church. However, the ceremony, which dates from a

feudal culture, together with the term 'interregnum', tends to inhibit the ideals of shared ministry and leadership. This effect has been modified in some ares by redesigning the accompanying liturgy in order to maximise lay participation and to highlight a new chapter in shared ministry.

244 Through Institution the incumbent has the backing of the wider Church to exercise the Church's ministry in a particular locality. He is free to do this either in an individualistic manner or in conjunction with churchwardens and PCC exercising 'pastoral care'. Indeed, wardens and PCCs are nominated in the *Synodical Government Measure* as the incumbent's chief helpers. The term 'pastoral care' needs to be interpreted in the light of the cultural and sociological background of each particular locality at any given time. The term 'pastoral' is at present normally interpreted to mean the care of individuals, whereas historically it implies the provision of appropriate leadership. Therefore, it may include what we now call 'mission' or 'evangelism' – the care of communities and individuals, so that people and situations may be transformed by the love of God in accordance with his will.

245 Many incumbents have already modified their understanding of these inherited institutions, and have used the authority already conferred to 'authorise' others to share in the work. However, in practice this remains a matter of goodwill. Although many bishops and their advisers try to ensure the continuity of shared ministry by the appointments they make, and attempt to come to an understanding with patrons, a new incumbent can decide to overturn any patterns of shared ministry he may have inherited. At present there is nothing in law that anyone can do to change the situation. This matter urgently needs to be examined with a view to making an incumbent accountable, as a condition of being appointed and of continuing to hold office, for accepting and implementing the policy arrived at by the bishop and PCC and their advisers.

246 However, the legal position has been considerably modified by the Pastoral Measure and while further changes in the law are being discussed the possibilities for shared ministry within the present framework should not be ignored. Some parishes have introduced 'eldership' or shared leadership schemes. These can be valuable provided that matters of authority and accountability are agreed between incumbent, wardens and PCC at an early stage and provided that the leadership

group promotes rather than inhibits a wider sharing of ministry and leadership.

Training for appropriate leadership

247　One of the most important keys to effect change is therefore the training of ordained and lay leaders in ways which help them to see their responsibilities in terms not only of providing, but also of stimulating, appropriate leadership for the Church in a fast-changing society. Perhaps the most significant feature of modern society is the revolution caused by the explosion of knowledge along with the expansion of education and literacy. This means that the function of leadership is to enable adults to become *interdependent* in decision-making rather than *dependent* on their 'superiors'. This situation affects not only the structures of the Church and styles of leadership, but also the way in which the activity and purpose of God is discovered within the world and society around the Church. Hence the importance of a *contextual* approach to theology, which makes demands on clergy and lay leaders very different from those for which they have traditionally been trained. It is necessary for them to move into a new culture of *learning* from situations and people rather than *teaching* and making decisions individually. Their own role becomes one of enabling a group to perceive the situation and issues about which they must make group decisions.

248　The curricula for theological colleges and courses need therefore to be geared more and more towards educating candidates in skills of stimulating local lay leadership, and of understanding and practising contextual theology. These are necessary for the continuing development of the inherited tradition in patterns of ministry and theology. In recent years, a number of initiatives have been taken in this direction. Over the last few years there has been a basic review of college curricula for clergy training under the provisions of ACCM *Occasional Paper* No 22.[19] Each theological college and course is now required to produce its own syllabus and method of assessment, within the parameters set by ACCM *Occasional Paper* No 22, and these must be related to an extensive statement about what the ordained ministry is for.

249　'Contextual theology' must not be understood or defined in such a way as to exclude the teaching of the Christian tradition. The emphasis in this report has been that of relating tradition to context. The ACCM Working Party Report *Ordination and the Church's Ministry: A Theological Evaluation* (1990) warns:

'There can be such an emphasis upon the action/reflection mode as a means of doing theology, that there is insufficient attention to the teaching of the Christian tradition as a medium for entering into knowledge of God.' (p. 24)

250   The BCC report *Partners in Practice* (1989) is of particular relevance when colleges and courses are trying to ensure that a fuller recognition of world mission issues are covered. The report has a particularly helpful final section on 'some leading questions' which raises questions not only on syllabus content but on staffing, feminist and racist topics, and ecumenical opportunities. All this involves looking at ministry in its relationship to faith, the Church and the world.[20] It is expected that there will be an emphasis on clergy as enablers of mission within the world, as well as of ministry within the church. To be this, as we have seen, they must be listeners as well as teachers.

251   Several colleges have set up centres in UPAs, where students can spend varying amounts of time learning to think theologically within a new situation.[21] These are often cross-cultural and multi-religious. Another way of providing similar exposure to new cultural contexts is through placements overseas, which an increasing number of students also undertake. Placements must not, however, be a substitute for seeking an interplay of theology and practice across the whole curriculum. Many of the new curricula also take seriously the fact that the Church itself, even within Britain, is a multi-racial and multi-cultural society.[22] Very important here is the setting up recently of the Simon of Cyrene Institute in London, for the development of Black Theology and Ministry. It is concerned with equipping laity and clergy, both black and white, to minister effectively in a multi-ethnic church.

Part-time training
252   Alternative patterns of training as provided by part-time courses have enabled the development of various forms of non-stipendiary ministry. Amongst these is the position of Minister in Secular Employment. This calling is not easy for candidates to envisage or sustain, and many who begin it end in the stipendiary ministry. However, there are real examples of how this form of ministry can enable mission, both in the work place, and in the parish, where an MSE can challenge his/her church to think more about the secular world in which most of its members work. Other examples of new developments are in the local ordination schemes being developed in one or two dioceses.

253 The rapid and radical nature of change, to which the Church needs to respond, highlights the same need as in other professions to provide for Continuing Ministerial Education. This is the In-Service Training, or even re-training, of existing clergy and accredited lay ministers. This will involve programmes designed in response to perceived need and providing the opportunity to experience and reflect on a number of situations, different from the participants' present sphere of work. Within this post-ordination training, as well as in initial training, help is needed to enable clergy to teach in a non-literate context and to operate with a collaborative style of leadership.

Clarifying the nature of ministry
254 New ways of developing the people of God are envisaged in *Faith in the City*, though it fails to note that nearly all the funds available for training and development are more geared to the further training of the clergy or for ordinand training than for other vocations in the Church. However, the grants from the Church Urban Fund are designed to encourage others. If we are to progress further we shall need to clarify the nature of ministry and the theological and organisational boundaries between the general ministry of all the baptised and that of the ordained. Many of these considerations apply to all churches in whatever setting. Perhaps the real and lasting importance of *Faith in the City* will be that by going to *listen* in the UPAs to the poor, the Church elsewhere is learning *how to hear* Good News in ways appropriate for sharing with *everyone*.

255 Both initial pre-ordination training and CME need to deal with the changing role of the church leader, as representative person in the Christian community. S/he is increasingly called to be a *corporate* sign of Good News of salvation within the world. Presumably the role is to exercise the kind of leadership noted above, but also to be a kind of watchman or *person on the boundary* between the Church and the rest of the world. The leader has to administer the Church or to make the necessary arrangements; s/he has also to be (as teacher, pastor or community worker) the facilitator – in the French idiom, the *animateur* – of the Church's life.[23]

The ability to cross boundaries
256 The leader's role in evangelism is therefore to be on the boundary, in order to assist the Church to cross boundaries. These may be in the geographical parish with its particular issues and possibilities, or in

particular fields, such as industrial mission, intellectual communities (e.g. universities, colleges and schools), or cross cultural situations. They may be religious or racial boundaries, or 'traditional' class boundaries.

Chapter 14

AUTHENTIC DISCIPLESHIP

A spirituality for every day

257 To develop an authentic 'spirituality of the *ordinary*' is a prime requisite if the Church is to become effective once again within our present society. The collection of essays *All are Called* gives a vision of each member of the Body of Christ being given due honour. It is a vision of the Church of the twenty-first century without 'first-class citizens', whether these be thought of as bishops, professors, nuns or social workers, and regardless of sex, age, race, wealth, intellectual ability – or ordination. But for this vision to be realised the *ordinary Christian vocation lived out in the world* has to regain its place at the centre of Christian concern.

258 Mark Gibbs (in an unpublished paper)[24] gives three signs of solidarity from the institutional Church and from fellow-Christians for which lay people long, when facing Monday's work, or unemployment, Wednesday night's political meeting or Saturday's leisure activities:

'(a) They long to be affirmed. That is they wish to be fully recognised as fellow-disciples of our Lord, although they do not work in Church structures. This is particularly true of those in 'hard' occupations, like trading and politics. The Churches often seem less supportive of these fellow-Christians than of those in 'caring' occupations like nursing or teaching or social work. It is extremely important that our liturgies and our worship shall constantly affirm that, irrespective of our jobs, or activities, or sex, or age, or anything else, God calls all of us.

'(b) They ask to be understood. That is they ask that theologians and clergy and other fellow-believers should take the trouble to examine the situations in which the laity find themselves and the complicated and powerful structures – some good, some evil – which may dominate their lives. This requires much sensitive and thoughtful probing of political and economic and social structures. And this must be done, not only for professional people, but for blue collar workers as well. There is certainly sometimes a wrong kind of Christian 'elitism' in

Christian thinking, though there may also exist a hidden bias which rejects middle class people out of hand. There has also been a good deal of sexist prejudice, too, examining the problems of lay*men* at work, and forgetting the employment of so many women in today's employment system.

(c) They must and do expect to be criticised, but only after they have been affirmed and their position has been understood, certainly not before. And in careful dialogue with them, and not from afar off. But none of us are exempt from the call to put our lives under the Gospel. In fact, though lay people may rightly resent blanket condemnations from church leaders and preachers, they may learn to appreciate frank criticisms from 'outside' their own structures – comments which they are sometimes not free to express themselves.'

259 Steps towards meeting these needs can be taken through liturgies and sermons, and through small groups, where open sharing is easier. Groups which meet in the work-place, or in homes or parish, meeting with or without the clergy may be more enabling. But many lay people are rarely into liturgies and sermons and are not attracted to groups. Before we consign them to self-chosen isolation, a further look at how we present Sunday worship and 'the parish programme', and how we 'lead laity' towards more varied and adventurous alternatives, bears examining. Is there a way of presenting the Gospel today which can plug into the felt needs of people? Is it true that there is a spiritual need and hunger in people which Christian spirituality best fills? Is the beginning of filling it affirmation or criticism?

The concept of discipleship

> Is there a way of presenting the Gospel today which can plug into the felt needs of people?

260 In a paper on 'Lay Spirituality' contributed to MTAG, Gwen Cashmore offers discipleship as a key concept – the idea of following and learning from Jesus Christ. Many people respect Jesus and what they know of his teaching – there is more difficulty for them with institutions and church people. To present Jesus, his way of life and the cost of discipleship in a way which is fresh and adventurous may trigger

responses. There are excellent programmes for renewing church people's discipleship – an example is 'Renew', a programme from the USA being used in some Roman Catholic dioceses, but we await programmes designed for people without specific church associations. Demand and challenge are features not to lose sight of. The recognition of the need for training, both for church people and others, is certainly central.

The concept of nourishment or nurture

---

261   Another current concept in wide use within our culture is *nourishment* or nurture. Josephine Bax in *The Good Wine* describes movements which can offer such nourishment from the Christian table – movements like Cursillo, the Retreat movement, networks connected with religious communities, Charismatic and Renewal Conferences and Centres. There are other resources for nourishment, too, whether connected with formal churches or not. Help in organising the nourishing disciplines of personal prayer and reading, and how to call on such resources in an ordinary working day, is also needed. Finding the way to offer such resources to non-churchgoing people, many of whom pray, would make Christian resources more accessible than offering only Sunday church services.

262   A model of the ordinary, shot through with new resources, points the direction. The pointers must not by-pass the family or the neighbourhood.

(a)   To claim that the basic ecclesial unit is the family seems either too obvious or too unrealistic. Many parents do not share religious conviction or practice and are embarrassed to participate in prayer in their homes with their families. However, the acceptance both of differences and of shared conviction in the home may well begin to rescue religion from individualism.

(b)   For many people neighbourhood relationships are still the stuff of life. Where a lived-religion is part of it, natural sharing of faith can happen unselfconsciously.

Articulating our faith

263   Many Christians have a lively personal religion which they do not know how to apply or express in the everyday world. Christian lay spirituality training must include help with *articulation skills*. On the whole it is the middle classes who are the least articulate about faith. Working class believers are more likely to talk challengingly about their faith at work, among mates, and in the locality. But many middle class people have been taught, or have discovered, that topics of conversation which arouse feelings, controversy or division are better avoided and that religion is one of these. Self-consciousness blights attempts to break out of this stranglehold. Simple faith-sharing exercises are needed to get atrophied muscles going, and the identifying of opportunities for speaking out the faith which motivates us. These can happen naturally when Christians are involved with others in working at issues like social analysis, sexual politics, inter-faith matters, educational policy – anything of sufficient importance to uncover deeply held conviction. They can happen in personal crises where feelings are shared mutually. It cannot happen when Christians are locked into narrow churchy clubs which separate them from ordinary people and force the Gospel to become nothing more than 'in-group' talk. How to encourage and train Christians out in the world to speak for Jesus, or in other ways to share faith, is a question of high priority. It will necessarily involve help in the listening skills.

> How to encourage and train Christians out in the world to speak for Jesus, or in other ways to share faith, is a question of high priority

264   Developing a spirituality of the ordinary; helping towards the proper affirmation, understanding and criticism of the laity; exploring the concepts of discipleship and nourishment – these are all increasingly seen as the natural tasks of lay Christians themselves, acting together. When they learn how to share their story and their experience of life, such sharing can lead to an individual discovering God in it all. It may lead to seeking God more through prayer and study. The witness of one may encourage another to faith in the God of their shared lives. The gap between 'spirituality' and ordinary life is one aspect of the way in which secular culture assigns religion to the private sphere. It is

therefore more likely to be crossed by Christians acting together. Honest sharing with each other is of prime importance therefore in learning to do this. The more Christians are able to build such bridges together between their work and their faith the more likely their contemporaries are to find common paths to wholeness.

Group life in the parish and beyond

265 Before becoming Southwark's Diocesan Missioner in 1972 Ivor Smith-Cameron was for some fourteen years Chaplain to the Imperial College of Science and Technology in London, where (he says) he learnt 'to evoke the Church in a secular society'. While recognising parishes and churches, and that the people within them develop knowledge and practice through training and application, he sees great value in networks of people working more independently of parochial structures to discover the Church in their work and secular setting so that by worship (including sacraments), fellowship, prayer and study they can reflect on and plan together their ministry in the world. Alongside and beyond such groups, he says 'there is little doubt that there is a large drop-out now among young women and men, who might have been involved in church-going in their early days, as they pass into adolescence and adulthood – but this must not mean that these women and men have ceased taking religion seriously'. He pleads that the churches offer a much wider range of opportunities for such people to share with others and express their faith in the common search.

266 After referring to Basic Christian Communities, particularly in the Roman Catholic communion in the Philippines, South America, Italy and Holland, Canon Smith-Cameron[25] writes:

'In Britain these groups do not necessarily share the same emphases as the Basic Christian Communities in other parts of the world, but we in the United Kingdom are also witnessing a burgeoning of groups. Let me suggest that in my own home almost every evening groups come together, at weekends they come together – their themes are much more concerned with taking seriously the ingredients of their daily life, their resources are essentially Holy Scripture. They wrestle with Scripture trying to work out in their daily life Gospel values, Gospel truths. They are less interested in ecclesial and ecclesiastical matters, important as these may be. For example, I doubt very much if the kind of group I am talking about will take very seriously the *Baptism, Eucharist and Ministry* document of the WCC. They will no be too concerned with the Lima document, or Local Ecumenical Projects or the Covenant Proposals, important as these things are. They will take much more seriously matters concerning justice, matters concerning peace, matters concerning martyrdom, matters concerning ecology, the environment, creation, redemption and they will try to work out how they "do" their theology – the praxis of theology. They will be more interested in trying to work out a Christology for Clapham, rather than enter into the details of the first four centuries' struggle in Christological understanding, not that they would think that was unimportant – a Christ for Clapham, rather than a Christ for Chalcedon.'

Action groups within the parish

267 The groups that met at Canon Smith-Cameron's house have been deliberately established *outside* parish structures, but groups with similar concerns *can* be established on a more overtly 'churchy' base. A common feature of many such programmes developing within churches in UPAs is that they grow out of people's sense of frustration. One good example is given in *Power to the Powerless – Theology Brought to Life* by Laurie Green (1987). This is the story of developments in his former parish in Erdington, Birmingham, lying under Spaghetti Junction on the M6. It tells how the hopelessness of many residents was transformed through fellowship and Bible study on the parables of Jesus into a practical vision of doing something constructive about their situation. They were a *Parables in Action* group learning to plan in order to respond to the real needs of the community. Action led to *reflection*, and then to renewed action and reflection and so on.

268 There were parallels, conscious or unconscious, with the Base Communities referred to by Ivor Smith-Cameron and mentioned on previous occasions in this report. The parallels with the Base Communities can however be overstated. Social concern in many of the English groups seems to have focused on relief of need, falling short of a radical questioning of social structures. There seems, too, to have been a greater dependence on paid, professional ministry than would be the case in many Base Communities in places such as South America, though this professional ministry has often seen its main role as being to produce local lay leadership.

269 In many suburban churches, too, there is a long tradition of house groups which mainly function as discussion groups. But it is crucial to recognise that a house group is not necessarily the equivalent of a Basic

Ecclesial Community, which is in effect a local church practising contextual theology, sharing a sacramental life and seeking to be faithful to a common vocation.

270   As was indicated in paras 216 *et seq*, small groups are also important for work among young people associated with a parish. Not only does their worship need to be accessible and understandable, spoken in the language and terms of today's youngsters. We need also to think more widely about the various ways there are of communicating the gospel better, using drama, music, videos and other arts in such a way as to make the very nature of the gospel clearer to them. For young people need to know the challenge of faith, the stories of Jesus' life, and what he actually said. They need to be clear in their own minds what the faith is, what it involves, and what it will cost them. In South Africa, where the Church has had clarity forced upon it by political urgency, young people have found their faith mirrored in the life of the Church, and have become the radical agents for change in the country as well as the most loyal of believers. We need to be equally clear what the demands of the gospel are in Britain today.

Ecumenical ministry

271   The cultural context in which mission is conducted is not simply an Anglican concern. It is relevant to all Christian traditions. Because the Church is faced in the Western world with a 'missionary' situation, the separate Churches are facing the same pressure that led, for example, in the Indian sub-continent to the formation of United Churches. However, attempts actually to unite the denominations in England (apart from the formation of the United Reformed Church) have so far dismally failed. Nevertheless, the impetus towards unity is strong and increasingly so, as the response of the Churches towards the Inter-Church process indicates.

Christian unity is a Sign of God's Kingdom

---

272   The passing of the *Ecumenical Relations Measure* and Canons by the General Synod is a further sign of the Church of England's commitment to work towards unity at the local level. The existence of about 600 Local Ecumenical Projects, in over three-quarters of which the Church of England is a partner, likewise testifies to the awareness that Christian

unity is a sign of God's Kingdom. LEPs are to be found in all areas of church life – where the churches are strong and where they are weak.

273   The church at Blackbird Leys on a deprived housing estate near the Cowley works on the edge of Oxford may be cited as an example of a typical LEP. Here the representatives of the Church of England, Baptist, Methodist and United Reformed Churches agreed that there should be one place of worship and ministry on the estate served by those four denominations together. So a church and adjoining halls were built. The norm is for there to be two ministers, one an Anglican priest and the other Free Church. Worship is always united. The congregation is multi-racial and multi-cultural. It sees its task as being to serve and challenge the community in every relevant way. A community worker is attached to the church and is based on the church premises. The gulf between the outlook of most residents and that of the church is so great that denominational differences are seen to be largely irrelevant to the mission of the Church. The only way of working that makes sense on this estate and in many other settings, is to worship and witness as the one people of God.

Three congregations reviewed

274   As will have been apparent to readers of this report a number of individual clergy and parishes have responded to our requests for information about how they are tackling the problems thrown up by the different cultural contexts in which they are placed. We have quoted from some of these already. Three parishes in particular were asked to provide much fuller accounts of their work. These disclosed great similarities as well as differences. They were asked to place in order of preference the following aims:

  to share spirituality
  to uphold and spread sound doctrine
  to raise awareness of social injustice
  to build up fellowship in the congregation
  to bring people to a personal experience of Jesus Christ
  to campaign for change in society
  to equip and nourish people for Christian discipleship in a secular world
  to offer community service to the locality
  to supply relief to the most needy.

275 One of the churches concentrated on bringing people into the felt reality of the Holy Spirit in the congregation and individually; the second on solid teaching and on evangelism through 'Christian information' courses and follow up; the third on a more open approach and discussion of contemporary issues. All three had house groups as well as Sunday worship; all valued fellowship in the congregation and the need to welcome newcomers; all provided for the nurture of children; all three had strong youth participation. All were in fact meeting the extended family needs of the mobile middle class and provided depth, purpose and direction to people directly serving in the enterprise culture or who, through their professions or in retirement, were servicing those who were. All congregations seem to include a group of less 'successful', less 'adequate' people, but this group was a small minority within the whole. The congregations were largely middle-class and relatively affluent.

> Living in the present structures while working to change them

276 Another feature of these congregations is that they provide a way for their members to express concern for the poor, while living within the present *status quo* in society. The generous private charity expressed financially and in prayer, concern and practical service for the poor, both overseas and at home, provides an outlet for Christian goodwill as well as for uncreative guilt. Even for the radicals in our churches who work for new levels of equality and justice for our society and the world, there is little alternative but to live within the present structures while they work to change them. Some in the Church may be discomfited by the recognition that the Church through its pension fund and clergy stipend arrangements is committed to and benefiting from the contemporary economic arrangements in society, having to balance awareness of ethical issues with the duty of trustees to do the best for their beneficiaries. From within this situation, Christian stewardship – tithing or an approximation to it – is a natural Christian response whatever other responses accompany it.

277 The Churches also provide opportunities for community building and personal service as an expression of Christian care. In some other places than those described – for instance, in market towns or where

the church is less specialised – the people in the parish around the church may have a more central place in the church's concern. This is an attitude which 'Mission Audit' encourages. In some places the parish church may still be the centre and focus of community life. In a fragmented society centres of community and vision are at a premium. If the church can avoid the pitfalls of paternalism and the offensive attitude of 'helping others' its many good works will be a sign of the Kingdom. The pitfalls are best avoided by the realisation that church people actually need their neighbours and that only by working with them for the good of the whole can their own needs be met.

278 When faced with the central questions which this Report raises, the churches differ in emphasis between acceptance and confrontation, direct challenge and dialogue, individual transformation and changing the structures. They would perhaps also divide on the theologies underlying world-affirming/world-denying attitudes, but in practice they would be accepting of the world as it is, while working hard to bring individuals around them to a deeper experience of life by pointing them to God's purposes in Christ. They varied in the amount of 'community work' they offered and in the degree to which they addressed contemporary problems, ethical and political, or worked for changes in society. How typical these congregations were of the modern urban Church readers' experience will help them decide. Readers will also decide in what direction they hope their own congregation will change in the next decade.

Conclusion
279 The relation between congregations of different allegiances, the attitudes of people to the Church and church-going, the goals and aims which congregations adopt (either deliberately or through inertia or custom) can be radically altered by changes in society. A government with a particular ideology, a new relationship with Europe or the Third World, a major disaster or fright, a strongly charismatic personality – all these may shake up and change attitudes and patterns of behaviour. But these are among the more unpredictable factors. There is an underlying trend to social change which continues despite the influence of such events. We have indicated in paras 22f what we believe this trend to be.

280 This analysis surely gives a new urgency for that kind of ecumenical witness which demonstrates that Christian convictions and

commitments differ from both prejudice and arbitrary dogmatisms. We have argued throughout this report that Christians are needed who will cross cultural boundaries, willing to listen and so enter into a genuine dialogue with others, rather than beating a drum from the safety of their own territory. Relying fully on God's grace, their continuing witness will be simple and quiet, until genuine opportunities for sharing their faith are given. Undemonstrative and sensitive witnessing does not mean being passive. As well as sharing the good news of Jesus with individuals and diverse communities, Christians are called to tackle the immense task of bringing to bear the Gospel message on the whole of modern culture. In so far as the accepted ideas and norms of culture do not recognise the loving graciousness and truth of God, Christians should be calling for a conversion which will lead to new attitudes and actions more in tune with the signs of God's Kingdom in the life of Jesus Christ. Whether witnessing to individuals, groups or culture as such, Christians will proceed humbly, respecting the human integrity of others and their responsibility both to make their own choices freely and to take the consequences for them. In the end they will give an account of their own lives to God, just as we will. The God revealed to us in Jesus Christ wants to save all human beings and bring together one new humanity through Christ. Before he can do this all will need to acknowledge the rightness of his judgement on our waywardness and pride. The church is called to be both a living sign and messenger of the Gospel for the sake of the healing of the nations.

Appendices

Appendices

GLOSSARY

ACCOMMODATION or ADAPTATION   The introduction of traditional western expressions of Christianity into other regions of the world, e.g. Asia, with some adjustment to local culture.

CONSCIENTIZATION   This rather ugly word was originally minted in relation to the South American scene and it refers to the process whereby people are made fully aware of their actual situation. It is the bringing into consciousness of the real facts of human existence. So, for example, St Peter's speech at Pentecost enabled his hearers to realise their responsibility and sinfulness and their consequent need to repent. Or, in South Africa, the conscientization of the blacks refers to their growing awareness of the extent to which the system of apartheid denies their essential humanity and to their recognition that this is not something inevitable, built into the order of things, but something that can be changed.

CONTEXTUALISATION   When used of Christian theology and worship this term denotes the rooting of the Gospel and its expression in a given locality. So while proclamation has to be grounded in the Bible, it has also to be related to the actual situation in which it is being made. In this sense contextualisation is virtually synonymous with indigenization (see below).

CULTURE   Culture is the compound of customs, priorities, values, assumptions and beliefs shared by a social group or community. It is therefore always historically conditioned and it is specific to particular localities, areas or countries and to particular times.

EVANGELISM
'Evangelism is the making known of the Gospel of the Lord Jesus Christ, especially to those who do not know it. It is a particular responsibility in the Church's mission. We are charged to communicate that the life, death and resurrection of Jesus Christ is good news from God. Evangelism usually involves the use of words but not inevitably so.

'It is essential that in evangelism the dignity of human beings is affirmed by giving them freedom to choose, without pressure. But of course there are many situations where it is right and proper for Christians to take the initiative appropriately and sensitively in making known the good news of Jesus Christ. Certainly it is the hope of evangelists that their hearers will be persuaded and come to faith'.

(The above abstract can be found as part of a fuller comment in *The Measure of Mission*, page 38f. Also in this publication are comments on the words Witness, Conversion, Proclamation, Dialogue, Proselytism, etc.)

The Lambeth Conference set evangelism in its four-fold definition of the Mission of the Church

'1. to proclaim the good news of the kingdom
2. to teach, baptise and nurture new believers
3. to respond to human need by loving service
4. to seek to transform the unjust structures of society'.

The Anglican Mission Agencies Meeting in Brisbane in 1986 related evangelism and mission as follows:

'The proclamation of Jesus Christ as the crucified and risen Lord and the confession that 'Jesus Christ is Lord' have both personal and cosmic implication. We cannot confess 'Jesus is Lord' without serious consequences for the ordering of the political and economic relationships of humankind and the harmony in which we live as part of the whole creation.'

EVANGELISATION
(Anglicans have been called to a 'Decade of Evangelism' while Roman Catholics have been called to a 'Decade of Evangelisation'. The second word includes the first, but is more comprehensive. The following paragraphs come from a paper prepared for the November 1990 meeting of the English 'Catholic Bishops' Conference'):

'Spreading the good news of the gospel is a task with many facets. The most common way this task is understood within our Catholic community is by the witness of one's own faith in Christ by example, in the situations of ordinary life. This witness is also expressed and made explicit by the sacramental and social celebration of the presence of God in the good and difficult things of life, and by action to bring Christian values to bear on the society in which we live. This last has the two-fold dimension of supporting and developing the situations in society which conform to the gospel, and challenging those which do not.

'This intimate connection between conversion, community and society is at the heart of Catholic belief about the Christian way. This is precisely the reason why we define evangelisation in terms which cover the whole range of activities from proclamation of Christ, to hearing the word, personal conversion to him, membership of his community, and action to bring his teaching alive in the world. We also emphasise the necessary connection between all the elements in the process. An emphasis on the *necessity* of the connection between the elements in the process is characteristic of evangelisation. Evangelism tends to stop with highlighting the first two or three.'

GOSPEL   The Gospel is the Good News of what God has done and is doing in and through Jesus of Nazareth. There is therefore a certain 'givenness' about it, since part of its content must bear witness to the life, death and resurrection of Jesus. But the application of this message together with witness to the continuing divine activity in the present can only take place in specific situations.

INCARNATION   It is central Christian doctrine that God has revealed himself to humankind for their salvation by coming among them as man. 'The Word was made flesh.' It is to this that *incarnation* (enfleshment) primarily refers. It can, however, be used in a derivative sense to refer to a parallel process whereby the Gospel is embodied in contemporary and local cultural forms. When evangelism and liturgy are understood in terms of incarnation (or of inculturation in the best sense) they have become truly indigenous expressions of Christianity.

INCULTURATION   *see* INCARNATION

INDIGENIZATION   This is a process whereby the expressions of Christianity (doctrinal statements, liturgies, church buildings, etc) correspond to the cultural forms of an area, without, however, eliminating the scandal of Christ. It is a continual process; there can be no final products because the societies in which we live are constantly changing.

SECULARISM   The belief that everyday secular life is completely autonomous and that nothing whatsoever is related to a divine being.

SECULARISATION   This is an ambiguous word but it is used in this report to denote separation from ecclesiastical control or from any relationship with religious institutions. A church school, for example, that has become a state school can be said to have been secularised. In itself the term implies no value judgement about the desirability or otherwise of the result.

MISSION THEOLOGICAL ADVISORY GROUP

List of Members

The Rev Canon Philip King (*Chairman 1985-1989*)
Acting Chairman on becoming Secretary to the Board for Mission and Unity
Brother Bernard, Society of St Francis
The Revd Professor J. Gordon Davies
Emeritus Professor of Theology in the University of Birmingham (died December 1990)
The Revd Prebendary John Gladwin (*until June 1989*)
Secretary, Board for Social Responsibility of the General Synod
Miss Margaret Jeffery (*from June 1989*)
Assistant Secretary, Board for Social Responsibility of the General Synod
The Very Revd Robert Jeffery
Dean of Worcester
The Revd Dr Andrew Kirk
Dean of Mission, Selly Oak Colleges, Birmingham
The Revd Dr Myrtle Langley (*until November 1989*)
Director of Training, Diocese of Carlisle
The Revd Mano Rumalshah (*until March 1989*)
Teacher at Edwardes College, Peshawar, Church of Pakistan. Formerly Vicar of St George's, Southall
The Revd Dr Andrew Wingate
Principal, College of the Ascension, Selly Oak, Birmingham

Consultant Observers

Fr John Ball, MHM
Mill Hill Missiological Institute
The Revd Dr Fergus Macpherson (*until December 1988*)
General Secretary, Conference for World Mission, British Council of Churches
The Revd Donald Elliott (*from March 1989*)
Commission Secretary, Churches' Commission on World Mission, Council of Churches in Britain & Ireland

Secretaries:

The Rt Revd Patrick Harris,
Partnership for World Mission; now Bishop of Southwell (until June 1988)
The Rt Revd John Neale,
Partnership for World Mission (from 1989)
The Revd Canon James Anderson,
Board of Mission

The Revd Professor J.G. Davies was a member of MTAG from its inception and died just before the Group held its final meeting to produce this report. Ever since his involvement in the WCC Study on the Missionary Structures of the Congregation, Professor Davies had a deep and perceptive view of the issues involved in mission. As a member of the Group he was always confrontational, constructive and able to help us all to see issues more clearly. He contributed much to this report and we would like to record our deep gratitude to him.

ACKNOWLEDGEMENTS

It would be impossible to list all those who have provided us with help, advice and resource material. We are grateful to them all. We should especially like to mention, however

Neville Black, Team Rector in Inner Liverpool; Adviser to the Diocese's Group for Urban Ministry and Leadership; and a Tutor on the Northern Ordination Course

The Revd Canon Christopher Bryant, Youth Officer, Peterborough Diocese

The Revd Canon Sehon Goodridge, Principal of the Simon of Cyrene Theological Institute

Jim Hart, Project Officer of the Evangelical Urban Training Project; a Member of the Institute of Housing

Dr Julius Lipner, Lecturer in Comparative Religions, University of Cambridge

NOTES

1 Newbigin, L. *The Other Side of 1984*, WCC 1984
  Newbigin, L. *Foolishness to the Greeks*, SPCK 1986
2 Pannenberg, W. *Christianity in a Secularised World*, SCM 1989
3 Berger, P. *The Heretical Imperative*, Collins 1980
4 Seddon, P. *The New Age: An Assessment*, Grove Books, 1990, p.11
5 Hart, J. *Creating Leaders in Working Class Communities: the Approach of the Evangelical Urban Training Unit*, EUTP
6 Leech, K. *Struggle in Babylon*, Sheldon 1988
7 *Prayers for a Decade*, CHP 1990
8 The late Sir Alister Hardy, formerly Professor of Zoology at Oxford, founded the Alister Hardy Research Centre in 1969
9 *The Measure of Mission*, CHP 1987, p.45
10 First published in *Crosscurrent*, Autumn 1988, National Society, and reprinted by permission of the Editor (also quoted by Colin Alves in *Free to Choose: The Voluntary Principle at Work in Education*, National Society 1991)
11 Eliot, T.S. *The Idea of a Christian Society and Other Writings*, Faber and Faber 1939
12 Shorter, A. *Toward a Theology of Inculturation*, Orbis/G. Chapman 1988, Introduction, p. xi
13 General Synod *Report of Proceedings*, Nov 1990 pp 1041-4
14 Gitari, D. 'Evangelism in Culture: Proclaiming Christ in Christ's Way' (Lambeth Conference 1988)
15 *Social Trends*, HMSO, Table 5.19, 1987
16 For a fuller discussion see Bunting, I.D. *Claiming the Urban Village*, Grove Booklets on Evangelism No. 6, 1989
17 Zizioulas, J. *Being as Communion: Studies in Personhood and the Church*, London 1985
18 *The Measure of Mission*, p.5
19 *Education for the Church's Ministry*, ACCM Occasional Paper No.22, 1989
20 *Partners in Practice, Report of Theological Educators*, BCC 1989
21 *Theology in Practice*, ACCM Occasional Paper No.29, 1988
22 Cracknell, K. & Lamb C., *Theology on Full Alert*, BCC 1986
23 Hull, J. *What Prevents Christian Adults from Learning*, SCM 1984
24 Mark Gibbs was a member of the Working Party which produced *All Are Called*. He was Director of the Audenshaw Foundation which produces the Audenshaw Papers concerned with the development of discipleship among Christian laypeople. He was one of the editors of the papers until his death and was author of many articles on discipleship.
25 Smith-Cameron, I. *Five Faces of the Church*, paper

BIBLIOGRAPHY

Besides those listed in the Notes (p.131) the following are referred to directly or indirectly in the text.

All Are Called. CHP 1985
*An Audit for the Local Church. BMU 1986
Baptism, Eucharist and Ministry. WCC 1982
The Church, H. Küng. Burns Oates 1967
Church and People in an Industrial City, E.R. Wickham. Lutterworth 1957
Constructing Local Theologies, R.J. Schreiter. SCM 1987
Encounter in the Spirit, A. Wingate. WCC 1988
Faith in the City, Archbishop of Canterbury's Commission on Urban Priority Areas. CHP 1985
Faith in the Countryside, Archbishops' Commission on Rural Areas. Churchman 1990
The Good Wine, J. Bax. CHP 1986
The Gospel in a Pluralist World, W. Pannenberg. SCM 1988
Jesus in our Western Culture, E. Schillebeeckx. SCM 1987
*Living Faith in the City, Archbishop of Canterbury's Group on Urban Priority Areas. General Synod 1989
Love the Stranger, R. Hooker and C. Lamb. SPCK 1986
New Religious Movements: A Practical Introduction, Eileen Barker. HMSO 1987
Not as the Scribes, L. Newbigin. SPCK 1987
Not Just for the Poor, Social Policy Committee of BSR. CHP 1986
Patterns for Worship, Liturgical Commission. CHP 1989
Power to the Powerless, L. Green. Marshall Pickering 1987
*Relations with People of Other Faiths. BMU 1986
A Rumour of Angels, P. Berger. Penguin 1970
Theology in the City, ed. A. Harvey. SPCK 1989
The Truth Shall Make You Free: The Lambeth Conference 1988. CHP for ACC 1988

*Books asterisked are available only through Church House Bookshop, 31 Great Smith Street, London SW1P 3BN (Tel. 071–222 5520)